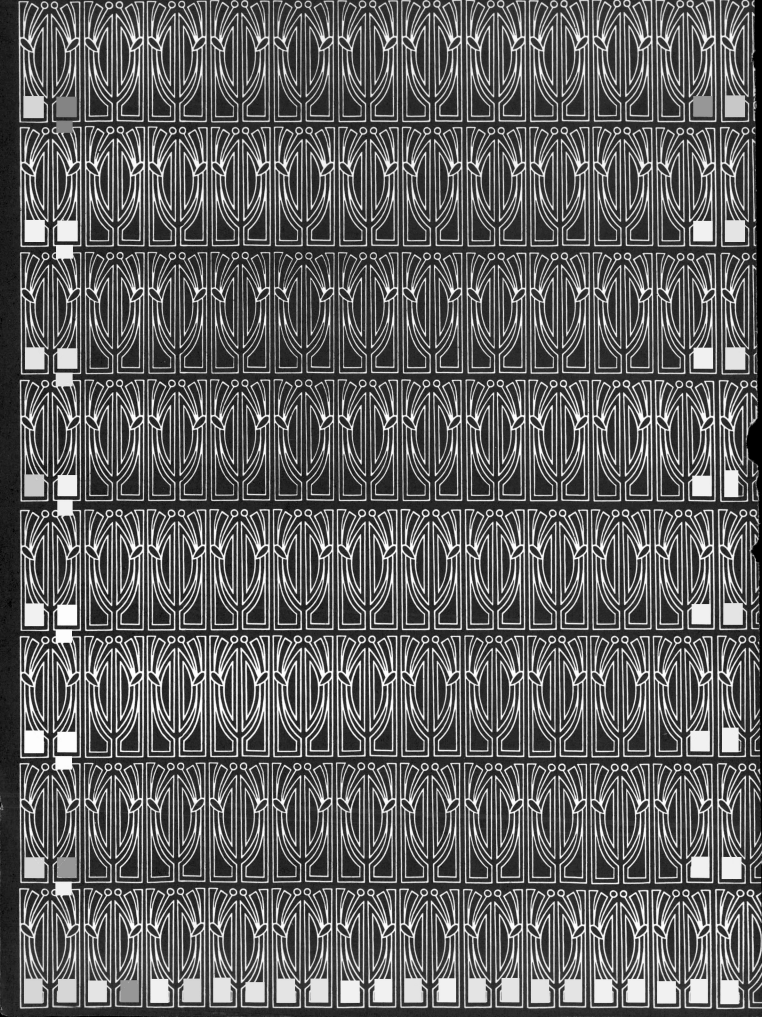

IN A GLAMOROUS FASHION

THE FABULOUS YEARS OF HOLLYWOOD COSTUME DESIGN

W. ROBERT LaVINE
Special Assistant and Photo Consultant, ALLEN FLORIO

CHARLES SCRIBNER'S SONS NEW YORK

"Moonlight Becomes You," by Johnny Burke and Jimmy Van Heusen. Copyright © 1942 by Famous Music Corporation; copyright © renewed 1970 by Famous Music Corporation.

Diana Vreeland's introduction to the catalogue for the exhibition, Romantic and Glamorous Hollywood Design, published by The Metropolitan Museum of Art, © 1974.

Photographic Sources

The Bad and the Beautiful, p. 122, from the MGM release *The Bad and the Beautiful* © 1952 Loew's Incorporated Inc. Renewed 1980 Metro-Goldwyn-Mayer Inc.

Bedtime Story, p. 60, copyright Columbia Pictures. Courtesy of Columbia Pictures.

Erté in his studio, p. 20, courtesy of Sevenarts Ltd. London.

Gilda, p. 110, copyright Columbia Pictures. Courtesy of Columbia Pictures.

Girl Crazy, p. 103, from the MGM release *Girl Crazy* © 1943 Loew's Incorporated Inc. Renewed 1970 Metro-Goldwyn-Mayer Inc.

The Great Ziegfeld, p. 86, from the MGM release *The Great Ziegfeld* © 1936 Metro-Goldwyn-Mayer Corporation. Renewed 1963 by Metro-Goldwyn-Mayer Inc.

His Kind of Woman, p. 201, courtesy of RKO General Pictures.

Irene Dunne in a Greer design for *Unfinished Business*, p. 63, courtesy of Universal Pictures.

The Joy of Living, p. 98, courtesy of RKO General Pictures.

The King and I, p. 134, © 1956 Twentieth Century-Fox Film Corp. All rights reserved. Courtesy of Twentieth Century-Fox.

The Monte Carlo Story, pp. 130 and 131, © 1957. United Artists Corporation. All rights reserved.

Oklahoma!, p. 133, © 1956 Twentieth Century-Fox Film Corp. All rights reserved. Courtesy of Twentieth Century-Fox.

Rhythm on the River, p. 47, courtesy of Universal Pictures.

Rita Hayworth with Jean-Louis, p. 109, copyright Columbia Pictures. Courtesy of Columbia Pictures.

The Swan, p. 238, from the MGM release *The Swan* © 1956 Loew's Incorporated Inc.

They All Kissed the Bride and Irene's sketch, p. 215, copyright Columbia Pictures. Courtesy of Columbia Pictures.

Two Weeks in Another Town, p. 132, from the MGM release *Two Weeks in Another Town* © 1962 Metro-Goldwyn-Mayer Inc., and John Houseman Productions, Inc.

West Side Story, p. 138, © 1962. Beta Productions, Inc. Released by United Artists Corporation. All rights reserved.

Zaza sketch, p. 208, courtesy of Universal Pictures.

Copyright © 1980 The Estate of W. Robert La Vine

Library of Congress Cataloging in Publication Data
LaVine, W. Robert
  In a glamorous fashion.
  1. Costume design—California—Hollywood—
History. 2. Costume designers—California—
Hollywood. I. Florio, Allen. II. Title.
  TT507.L36   791.43'026'0979494   80–16512
  ISBN 0–684–17661–0

1 3 5 7 9 11 13 15 17 19   Q/P   20 18 16 14 12 10 8 6 4 2

Printed in the United States of America

Opening page: Marlene Dietrich en route to England to make Knight Without Armour *(1937; photograph probably 1936).*

For Cecil Beaton —

with gratitude and affection —

Acknowledgments

When I took Bob La Vine, or Ace, as he was known to many of his friends, to the doctor that Monday morning in July 1979, he had all intentions of coming back to his apartment. He left his work area as though he would return in a few minutes, as was his habit. Yet leaving things undone was not characteristic of him. Having been closely related to Mr. La Vine in many aspects of his life, and now administrator of his estate, I was very clued in about the facets of this book. I had a good idea of what was still to be done and of what was incomplete. I also knew whom he would want to thank for having assisted him in making the book a reality.

I wish to acknowledge and especially thank the following people, some of them friends, for having made Bob's dream possible:

Richard Adams, for proffering so unselfishly his technical and legal expertise;

Jim Berry, for his artistic sense and suggestions, his superb photos, and his unbounded enthusiasm for the book's success;

Terri Cremin, for the myriad copies she made and the hours of dictation she took, as well as for her untiring desire to contribute her time and services;

Allen Florio, for his zest and determination in tracking down rare stills, for his deep knowledge of the cinema, but most of all for his support and for his stepping in at a very difficult time;

Bill Kenly, for the use of his still library, and for his expertise in movie lore;

Joe Pool, for his unstinting help and support in many areas that left Bob free and unhampered to pursue his book's development;

Ed Rathke, for his constant support, and for his listening to and understanding Bob's ideas.

To all the Hollywood personalities with whom Bob personally spoke, for volunteering their time and anecdotes and adventures, a heartfelt thank you.

To the many people and organizations—Ronald Alter, Howard Mandelbaum, *Movie Star News,* Viola Fafangel, Betty Jones, Joseph Yurasits, the late Merle Oberon, Edith Head, Bob Mackie, Stella Blum (curator of the Costume Institute at the Metropolitan Museum of Art, New York), and Eileen Hose (secretary to the late Sir Cecil Beaton)—an equally sincere thank you.

Bob's gratitude would also go to the many friends who contributed suggestions; to the major studios for the use of important stills, with special thanks to Ben Carbonetto and to Lou Valentino for their encouragement and contributions.

Lastly, at Scribners, special thanks to Katherine Heintzelman for her invaluable help in obtaining permissions; and to Bob La Vine's editor, Mrs. Patricia Gallagher, who succeeded in preserving in this book Bob's true spirit and manner of writing—"in a glamorous fashion"—go his and my deepest gratitude.

ROBERT PRAIRIE

Glamorous and romantic Hollywood design. The glorification of heroes and heroines. Beautiful women, handsome men. Everything was larger than life. The diamonds were bigger, the furs were thicker and more. The silks, velvets, satins and chiffons, and miles of ostrich feathers. Everything was an exaggeration of history, fiction, and the whole wide extraordinary world.

The basis was perfect designing and incredible workmanship—the cut of décolletage, the embroidery, the mounting of a skirt, and miles and miles of bugle beads.

The eye travelled, the mind travelled, in a maze of perfection and imagination.

DIANA VREELAND

CONTENTS

FOREWORD

IT IS TRUE THAT HOLLYWOOD INTRODUCED A NEW SENSE OF FASHION AND beauty to the world, and, sad to say, also true that the designers of the clothes worn by the famous Hollywood film stars were never really given their full credit.

This book is dedicated to putting that right and nobody was more fitted than Mr. Robert La Vine to do so. I worked with him many times on designs for films and plays. His infectious enthusiasm made these assignments a pleasure, and I was always impressed by his extensive knowledge of costume and fashion, particularly in the context of Hollywood.

Here Mr. La Vine has brought to our attention fascinating details, forgotten or probably never known by some, of Claire West's costumes for D. W. Griffith's *Intolerance;* the great influence of the French couturier, Paul Poiret, on the work of American film designers; Natacha Rambova's designs for *Camille* and *Salomé.* Among the other earlier designers, we learn of the work of Paul Iribe and Erté; and we are reminded of such stars as Lillian Gish, Marion Davies, Clara Bow, Gloria Swanson, and Pola Negri.

The movies played a great part in people's lives from the thirties onwards. We all went to the cinema once or twice a week; Marlene Dietrich, Jean Harlow, Joan Crawford, Norma Shearer became familiar names; we sat in the dark entranced by their dramatic portrayals on the "silver screen"; we were dazzled by their glamorous dresses, but perhaps we took these for granted and gave only a fleeting thought to the skill and effort that went into creating them. Imagine, for instance, and marvel at in retrospect, the dress worn by Marlene Dietrich in *Angel* in 1937, made of rubies, emeralds, topazes, and diamonds, a confection from the talent of Travis Banton, Paramount's own designer and one of the most important of the golden years of Hollywood.

Adrian, MGM's chief man, among his many great achievements helped to make Garbo on the screen unforgettable—off the screen, too, when he persuaded her to appear at a party dressed in a black velvet doublet as Hamlet.

Edith Head, still the chief designer at Universal, has had a long and distinguished career and has been responsible for the costumes of many memorable films in the forties and fifties, *The Heiress, All About Eve, Roman Holiday, To Catch a Thief.*

These talented people, together with many others like Orry-Kelly, Helen Rose, Walter Plunkett, and Irene Sharaff, have made superb contributions to a number of excellent films—*Casablanca, Gone With the Wind, The King and I, Cat on a Hot Tin Roof*—and have helped to make film costume design a fascinating art form.

For the last twenty years now, Academy Awards have been given purely for costume design, a fitting acknowledgement. It is gratifying to me, personally, that this honour was first granted to Mme Karinska, a Russian designer of supreme quality. Since then, of course, well-deserved Oscars have been awarded to many of the great Hollywood film designers.

As in the early days of films, the influence, wholly for good, of French couture continues to be strong: the work of Givenchy on dresses for Audrey Hepburn, for example, and of Pierre Cardin, Balmain, and Schiaparelli.

Despite the revolution of television and its all-absorbing popularity, films made in the big studios of Hollywood, and on location all over the world, are still exciting entertainment. With sensational advances in technique, wide screens, three-dimensional effects, and the extraordinary wealth of expertise gathered over the years from the twenties to the present day by hundreds of skilled people in the industry, the cinema will always be a dramatic force; and, happily, film costume designers have carved their place in history. They have created style; they have wrought magic and glamour in our lives; they have ensured that film costume design is now a subject of serious study for design historians, manifesting itself in interesting books, like this one, and in imaginative exhibitions in countless places, keeping alive the great tradition of Hollywood.

CECIL BEATON
November 1979

PART ONE

THE
SETTING

The Early Twentieth Century

THE BEGINNINGS OF AN INDUSTRY

MOVIES BEGAN IN THE EARLY 1890s WITH THE INTRODUCTION OF PRIMITIVE, hand-cranked machines that ran short filmstrips. By turning a crank and peering through an eyepiece in one of the new devices, a viewer could see flickering images of humans and animals in motion. However, astonishing as they were these creations were little more than elaborate peep shows offered in penny arcades for the low-salaried working classes. Then in 1895 the French Lumière brothers introduced a simple film projector that could handle two-reel films—and the fun began.

Adolph Zukor, an emigrant from Hungary who had become a successful furrier in Chicago before moving to New York, recognized the potential of the *frères* Lumière projector. In 1902, Zukor took a gamble and transformed a small New York loft on Fourteenth Street at Union Square above the Crystal Arcade, calling it Crystal Hall. Inside, for the first time, audiences sat on folding wooden chairs arranged in rows to watch the new rage, "moving pictures," to the accompaniment of a tinny upright piano. Musical scores were pieced together by the performer, who played excerpts from classical scores, selected to underline the action of the film being shown above the piano.

Zukor's daring venture proved successful, and similar crude movie houses began sprouting up in store fronts and small factory lofts everywhere.

The first cinematic narrative appeared in 1903, when Edwin Porter made a short film entitled *The Life of an American Fireman.* The mini-drama showed a fire alarm sounding, firemen leaping from their beds and sliding down the brass pole in the firehouse, and the triumphant rescue of a woman and her child from a burning house. Later that year, Porter produced and directed *The Great Train Robbery,* extending and refining the storytelling principles he had already established, in a tale about cowboys and bandits in the Far West—a formula that exists even today. The film became a classic, and for years afterward was the standard premiere attraction shown when a new movie theater opened.

Other showmen immediately began to form production companies, and by 1910 Vitagraph in Brooklyn, Essanay in Chicago, and Biograph in New Jersey were busy supplying growing audiences with "flicks." D. W. Griffith, who had founded Vitagraph in 1909, was responsible for many innovations in this new medium. From a technical standpoint, Griffith's 1916 *Intolerance* was a particularly important film. For the first time in an American movie, lavish sets were built and period costumes were made for thousands of extras; scenes varied from the palace of Belshazzar to the slums of a modern city and, finally, Calvary. Obviously influenced by the films of Italian filmmakers Giovanni Pastrone (*Fall of Troy,* 1910), Giuseppe de Liguoro (*The Inferno,* 1910), and Enrico Guazzoni (*Mark Antony and Cleopatra,* 1913), Griffith's mammoth undertaking contained elaborate spectacles the theater had never been equipped to offer.

A significant event that would elevate movies to the big time occurred in 1912. Against the advice of his colleagues, Zukor paid forty thousand dollars for the rights to a four-reel French-produced film version of *Queen Elizabeth,* starring the renowned Mme Sarah Bernhardt in a celluloid re-creation of her famed stage version of the life of England's Virgin Queen. Asked why she had agreed to participate in the new medium of film, the sixty-seven-year-old actress replied that she foresaw it to be "my one chance for immortality."

For the film she wore the costumes she had commissioned from Paul Poiret, the leading couturier in Paris at the time. A supreme egotist, Poiret flourished at a time when Paris was the uncontested center of art and beauty. More than fashion innovations, Poiret's creations were often controversial apparel *inventions,* sweeping away the remaining fragments of the faded *belle époque* mode and setting the stage for the defiant fashion revolution of the approaching twenties. Poiret was surrounded by the avant-garde artists of Paris. He was a patron of the painters Raoul Dufy and Pablo Picasso, and of the young poet Jean Cocteau; an employer of the Russian émigré designer Roman de Tirtoff (later known as Erté), and a friend of the American dancer Isadora Duncan, the architect Le Corbusier, and the talented photographer from New York Edward Steichen. Both Dufy and Picasso designed a number of printed silks for Poiret, which served as cushion covers and curtains for a barge moored in the Seine in Paris, where he gave *intime* supper parties and retreated from the feverish world of Parisian society.

For Bernhardt's *Elizabeth,* Poiret adopted the romantic Italian Renaissance

The flamboyant French designer Paul Poiret entitled his autobiography King of Fashion. *He was also called "King of Paris" and "Rajah of the Faubourg Saint-Honoré" by his disciples; modesty was never one of his strong points. His genius revolutionized fashion by bringing a new form of beauty, steeped in Orientalism, to women.*

The legendary Sarah Bernhardt acted in Queen Elizabeth *(1912), wearing costumes designed by Paul Poiret. This photo was used for the first movie poster.*

styles rather than the more accurate farthingales and severely fitted bodices of the English Tudor period. He replaced the near-architectural mode of the Elizabethan Age with high-waisted soft gowns worn with flowing capes. Bernhardt's dresses were accented by immensely wide, draped oversleeves, high curved and wired Medici collars of thick lace, and tiny neck-ruffs. Poiret's flair for the theatrical served Mme Sarah so well she also asked him to dress her for the 1912 film version of *Adrienne Lecouvreur*, released in America with the rather elongated title *An Actress's Romance Under Louis XV, In Three Parts*.

Extravagant and original, Poiret had surrendered to the visual excesses of the Ballets Russes (brought to Paris by the audacious Russian impresario Sergei Dia-

Léon Bakst's sumptuous drawing of his costumes worn by Ida Rubinstein and Nijinsky in Schéhérazade, first performed in Paris in 1910 by Diaghilev's Ballets Russes. A total work of art, this harem tragedy concerning the love of the sultan's favorite for her slave had an instant and overwhelming impact on Parisian audiences. It released a flood of barbaric splendor and scintillating color, causing the young poet Jean Cocteau to rhapsodize, "The curtain rises on festivities that shake up France and draw Dionysus's chariot."

ghilev in the spring of 1909). The dancing of Karsavina, Nijinsky, Pavlova, the superb décor and costumes of Bakst, Korovine, and Roerich, the thrilling music of Borodin, Rimsky-Korsakov, and Tchaikovsky, combined in romantic and exotic fantasies, left audiences gasping. The poet Anne de Noailles said of the event, "Everything dazzling, intoxicating, enchanting, seductive had been assembled and put on the stage."

Later, when the Diaghilev company debuted in London, J. B. Priestley would write that "they burst on London like a bomb filled with silks and coloured lights," and Lady Diana Cooper said: "Never since we have had our eyes so blinded with new light. The comets whizzed across the unfamiliar sky, the stars danced." Léon Bakst's designs for *Nuit d'Egypte* with the statuesque Ida Rubinstein as Cleopatra caused a sensation about which Jean Cocteau would write: "She was lifted by six black slaves from a chest of gilt and ebony, a swathed mummy, and the slaves unwound a series of brilliantly coloured veils to reveal the glorious figure of Cleopatra. She stood before the breathless audience, penetratingly beautiful like a great pungent perfume of some exotic essence." Diaghilev brought *Schéhérazade* to the Théâtre National de l'Opéra a year later, with Nijinsky dancing the role of the Golden Slave. This superb combination of music, choreography, and Bakst's settings and costumes changed theatrical concepts of the period and engendered what was later known as the Ballets Russes style.

The exoticism Diaghilev unleashed on the West inspired Poiret to create his *mode orientale*. He cut women's dinner gowns into the shapes of lampshades, draped their heads with striped silk turbans sprouting egret feathers held in place by barbaric jewelry set with paste emeralds and rubies, and made kimonos into evening wraps. Ankle-tight hobble skirts, short minaret-shaped tunics, and belts as wide as a Japanese obi were modeled by his exotic models in his salon at 37 rue Pasquier, and it was not long before Poiret's startling new interpretations of Diaghilev's splendor found their way onto the movie screens of pre–World War I America. The sultan's favorite in *Schéhérazade* preceded the movie vamp, and in 1932 Adrian would turn to this period of Poiret's work for inspiration when he costumed Garbo for MGM's *Mata Hari.*

With his daring design, love of fantasy, and unbridled use of extravagant materials, Poiret created garments that were more often costumes than haute couture. He once proclaimed, "I freed the bosom and gave liberty to the body." He had, in fact, invented the brassiere in 1912, and it was this liberation of a woman's body from stiff, painful corseting that allowed a new eroticism in dress. The fabrics Poiret made fashionable—embroidered Chinese silk, crêpe georgette, patterned metallic lamé, satin handpainted with exotic designs, soft leathers cut and punched out to imitate lace, thread-of-gold and silver appliquéd motifs—helped create the mystique of *luxe* surrounding movie stars during the twenties and thirties. During those decades, the finest movie costumers were, in a sense, disciples of Poiret. Natacha Rambova, Howard Greer, and Adrian all either worked or studied in Paris when Poiret was still an important fashion arbiter, and both Travis Banton and Orry-Kelly have acknowledged their admiration of his work and his influence on them. Erté, who had worked as an assistant to Poiret before World War I, certainly showed the influence of his early employer when he designed for MGM in 1925.

Poiret never designed for the American studios, although when he visited Hollywood in 1928 he was approached by an emissary of William Randolph Hearst to dress Marion Davies for a film. Instead, he chose to return to Paris—

Theda Bara in Cleopatra *(from Famous Players-Lasky, 1917). Unfortunately, the costume designer is not known. The nightclub-Egyptian décor served perfectly as a background for La Bara's gown and the entire pastiche knocked 'em out at the corner-storefront movie house. The spectacular had arrived!*

This 1913 drawing of Paul Poiret's lampshade gown "Sorbet" was the inspiration for a gown that Cecil Beaton designed for the famous Ascot scene in My Fair Lady (1964).

The imperious Pola Negri demanded that Paramount's Howard Greer spare nothing when it came to her costumes. In The Cheat *(1923),* Pola played the role of an ambitious Long Island housewife trying to further her struggling husband's career by serving his boss and wife a simple little home-cooked meal. This is the way Pola looked when the boss arrived: in elaborate arabesques of seed pearls and an embroidered front panel that featured the famed Iribe rose. For good measure Greer threw in a black bird-of-paradise fan and looped the star's tresses with ropes of pearls and jewels. Hubby received the promotion.

where he died, impoverished and forgotten, in 1944. Poiret's influence on motion picture costume design has been inestimable, and one can only surmise what fascinating garments he might have produced had he turned his extraordinary talents toward a movie camera.

In the 1920s, women's faces also changed to suit the new, mysterious look. Replacing the valentine smile of vacuous innocence worn like a mask by women of polite society during the early 1900s, women now affected a drawn paleness and a near-cynical stare of contempt and boredom. With their faces flattened by white clown's powder and their eyes heavily outlined with black kohl, fashionable Parisian and American women hinted of lurking evil. It was the first time in history that mass dieting among women became popular, and with it the happily rounded figure of the nineties disappeared. The day's ideal became a shocking new creature, thin to the point of emaciation, called the femme fatale: a heartless but irresistible woman who exploits men by the unscrupulous use of her sexual allure.

Dozens of such seductresses enthralled movie audiences for years. One of the most sensational was Theda Bara (formerly Theodosia Goodman from Cincinnati, Ohio), who in 1915 popularized the vamp in America. Within three years she appeared in more than forty movies bearing such provocative titles as *The Serpent, The Eternal Sin, A Fool There Was, Destruction,* and *The She-Devil.* Other vamps included Pola Negri, Barbara La Marr, and Mae Murray. Perhaps the most famous femme fatale in films was the beautiful but deadly Mata Hari, as portrayed by the great Garbo. Certainly one of the most fascinating femmes fatales was the famed Nazimova, a Russian-born actress, who had played Ibsen and Chekhov on the New York stage with great success.

In 1922, billed as "The Great Nazimova," she announced she would produce and star in a film version of Oscar Wilde's lurid poetic drama *Salomé*. Nazimova's choice of a vehicle to display her extraordinary talents was a daring one. Originally written in 1892 for Sarah Bernhardt, *Salomé* was declared too immoral for the Parisian stage, and on the eve of its first performance in London, with the sets painted and the polished brass braziers of perfumed incense ready to be lighted as a signal for Bernhardt's entrance, censors there, too, prevented the curtain from rising.

For *Salome,* Nazimova chose Natacha Rambova (born Winnifred Shaughnessy of Salt Lake City, Utah), a young socialite and designer, to create both sets and costumes. Twenty-five years old, beautiful, rich, and audacious, Rambova perhaps typified that group of post-debutantes in the twenties who dabbled in various art forms, usually to little effect.

Asked by a newspaper reporter how she envisioned Salome, Rambova replied, "Like a living pearl, precious but cold, her veins throbbing with quick-silver instead of blood." She convinced Nazimova that Aubrey Beardsley's 1894 art nouveau illustrations for Wilde's play ought to serve as the design inspiration for the film, and ultimately, the compatible marriage of motifs from Beardsley and Rambova's "art moderne" style resulted in an extraordinary visual experience. Rambova's daring conception and masterful use of the black-and-white

Drawing of the beautiful designer Natacha Rambova in 1927.

medium to depict Wilde's dramatic poem included a palace of endless arches, unexpected staircases that led to nowhere, and screens patterned with stylized lilies and writhing vine tendrils.

In Rambova's costumes, Nazimova moved like a creature in a hothouse of festering evil, a figure in a Hieronymus Bosch painting. In one scene her hair was frizzed like a seeding milkweed pod and stuck with pigeon-egg pearls, and she wore a simple white tunic like that of a girl in a convent. In another, her slight, childlike body was tightly bandaged to the knees with silk and draped with strands of pearls, and a fan of white egret feathers quivered on her head. She appeared on the terrace of the palace wearing a turban and a narrow cape that flowed downward to form a vast curved train, decorated with bold oriental arabesques borrowed from motifs Serge Soudeikine had used when he had dressed Karsavina as Salome for the Diaghilev ballet in 1913.

For Salome's Dance of the Seven Veils, Rambova swathed Nazimova in chiffon veils and covered her head with a startlingly simple white lacquered wig. In contrast to the central character, the others—Herod, Salome's mother, the members of Herod's court, servants, eunuchs, and guards—were transformed into deadly night-insects who swarmed about the princess of death, eager for the kill. For 1922 movie audiences, accustomed to flowery romances or circus-like biblical dramas, it was a heady, shocking spectacle.

This fantastic headdress was designed by Rambova for Nazimova in the film version of Salome *(1922).*

"The Peacock Cape," one of the series of art nouveau illustrations done by the English artist Aubrey Beardsley for Oscar Wilde's drama Salome. *First published in 1894, Beardsley's strange drawings were thought erotic and caused a scandal.*

Rambova's celebrated contempt for budgets and lack of restraint in money matters usually resulted in the studios' staggering under the weight of tremendous expenditures for the films she was involved in. But as far as design was concerned, her costumes and sets were magnificent. Unfortunately, her brilliant career as a designer for films was overshadowed by her highly publicized and tumultuous marriage to Rudolph Valentino in 1922—a marriage that ended in divorce only a few years later.

In recent years, Nazimova's portrayal of Salome has received the questionable stamp of high camp, but it remains one of the most original design conceptions in early Hollywood production. Rambova was not only one of the most inventive designers who ever worked in films, she was also a strong influence on those who followed her into and beyond the twenties, and along with Paul Iribe, Erté, and Cecil Beaton, she was one of the few artists entrusted with creating both the costumes and the sets for a film.

During the early years of film making, most production companies were located in the New York area. Costuming was arranged by the actresses themselves or clothes were bought at local department stores or from Broadway costume-rental houses. Those fortunate actresses who had extensive wardrobes of their own received more parts than more modestly dressed women. Most films at the time required only one or two ensembles, perhaps with changes of accessories and costume jewelry. The point was to "make do" when it came to dressing for a film, and most films were hodgepodges of apparel. In the more elaborate productions of D. W. Griffith and Cecil B. De Mille that required period costuming, garments were quickly made for the stars and principals, and the supporting cast and extras were garbed with either rented clothes or hastily assembled odds and ends of circus or masquerade paraphernalia. For contemporary roles, stars wore their own couture gowns; Pola Negri appeared in Callot, Worth, and Vionnet creations. Ina Claire favored Molyneux and Chanel, and Edna Mayo and Irene Castle turned to Lucile.

One of the earliest costumes specifically made for a film actress was created by French director Louis Gasnier for Pearl White in *Mysteries of New York* (1918). The outfit was a simple black velvet two-piece suit with a white silk blouse and narrow black ribbon tie, complemented by a black velvet beret. This ensemble proved so attractive that secretaries and shop girls copied it, and Gasnier's design became a kind of middle-class-working-girl's uniform.

Natacha Rambova adapted Beardsley's illustration for the film Salome. *Rambova's thrilling designs remain among the most extraordinary examples of costumes ever created for black-and-white films.*

Rambova's whimsy and sensibility are nowhere more evident than in her costume sketches. This delightful design was made for a guest in the masquerade ball scene of Cecil B. De Mille's Saturday Night *(1922). A bewildering concoction of ribbons, petals of varicolored chiffon, tassels, jewels, sequins, and embroidered lace, Rambova's creation reflects the influences of the Ballets Russes and Parisian revues that she had seen in France. The doll-face makeup was typical of the 1920s.*

As art director of The Young Rajah (from Famous Players-Lasky, 1922), Natacha Rambova insisted that Rudolph Valentino (her husband) and his leading lady be draped in ropes of pearls and covered with jewel-encrusted metallic cloth. Though the film's expensive costumes and sets impressed audiences with their Schéhérazade-like splendor, Valentino's fans rejected the scenario as nonsense.

Rambova's ultramodern costumes and art direction for Camille (Metro, 1921) created a sensation in Hollywood. It starred Nazimova and Valentino.

Natacha Rambova and Rudolph Valentino: Los Angeles, 1925

Into the Twenties

THE CREATION OF HOLLYWOOD

BY THE MID-TWENTIES MOST OF THE IMPORTANT FILM COMPANIES HAD either moved to Hollywood or originated there. Louis B. Mayer, a shoemaker, joined with Sam Goldfish (later Goldwyn), a glovemaker, to form Metro-Goldwyn-Mayer. The Warner brothers, who had started with a nickleodeon peep show on New York's Fourteenth Street, founded the studio that bears their name. Adolph Zukor, an ex-furrier from Chicago, headed Paramount Pictures.

Southern California became the movie mecca for a number of reasons. It was far from the cold weather found in the East and close to Mexico, a place where film producers felt they could escape the worldwide monopoly of the Motion Pictures Patents Company, a consortium of American and French moviemakers that legally controlled all film production. The location also provided the studios with plenty of cheap labor.

The development of costume design departments in the Hollywood studios was the result of two major factors: There were few fashion sources to draw on in California, and special costumes were needed for the epics, period stories, musicals, and Westerns that became staples of the industry. The Western Costume Company, on Melrose Boulevard in Hollywood, rented to the studios from their large stock of period and folk costumes, but this proved in time to be an expensive and often imperfect way of dressing a film.

Studios had wardrobe departments, in early days rather inadequate but none-theless important to the making of films. There costumes were hastily assembled, and extras lined up to receive their disguises each morning and return their borrowed outfits when the workday ended. Each wardrobe department had a head of wardrobe and a small staff of workers. Although alterations and repairs were made to the meager collections of costumes assembled from downtown Los Angeles bargain racks, no attempt to design costumes from a sketch was made in the early days of the studios.

Cecil B. De Mille was one of the first film directors to realize the importance of talented scenic and costume designers to a more advanced kind of movie production. De Mille, who would become Diaghilev's counterpart in the Hollywood movie world, had moved to California from New York, where he had been a successful theatrical producer-director and sometime playwright. Working out of Paramount, De Mille established an image of unrelenting extravagance for that studio, quickly setting new standards for other studios. He was intrigued by the limitless production possibilities offered by the movies, and his flamboyance and daring made him an instant legend.

De Mille's films never failed to provide audiences with a visual feast that was only obtainable on the screen, and his extravagances were fully publicized to create an image of studio largess. Elaborate bathtub scenes that first shocked, then delighted audiences became a De Mille trademark. (After Claudette Colbert languished in an alabaster pool filled with asses' milk as the Roman courtesan Poppea in Paramount's 1932 biblical extravaganza *The Sign of the Cross,* a leading American cosmetics manufacturer revived his depression-struck industry by introducing bubble bath to millions of women who longed for a touch of movie luxury.)

De Mille always demanded and got the best. He gathered around him a staff of talented writers, designers, and other artisans. Jeanie Macpherson, whom he met in 1914, became both his scenarist and mistress. She described him as a "funny little tornado." For his costume designer, De Mille chose the versatile Claire West, who had designed *Intolerance* in 1916 for D. W. Griffith. Miss West's often outré creations delighted De Mille as well as his stars—Gloria Swanson in particular. Better than any other designer with whom he would work, West supplied him with one of the major ingredients for his recipe for successful movie magic: "sex, sets, and costumes."

In 1919, De Mille directed *Male and Female,* an adaptation of Sir James Barrie's stage success *The Admirable Crichton.* For this film, De Mille insisted that Adolph Zukor bring the artist-designer Paul Iribe from France to create the sets and costume his leading lady, Gloria Swanson. By accepting De Mille's demand for a major artist as his production's designer, Paramount became the first studio in Hollywood to acknowledge the importance of creating special costumes for its stars. Claire West and the young designer Mitchell Leisen (later a noted director) provided the wardrobe for the supporting cast. De Mille, incidentally, also used the services of two other young unknowns for that film—a student dancer named Martha Graham, and a sketch artist who helped lay out the advertisements, eighteen-year-old Walt Disney.

In a flashback scene in *Male and Female,* Miss Swanson was seen as a haughty princess in the ancient court of Babylon. For this exotic sequence Iribé gave her a costume made almost entirely of pearls and she was crowned with a jeweled white peacock's head displaying a fortune in white egret feathers. The film's sets and costumes equaled Swanson's performance for sheer tour-de-force spectacle, and established De Mille as the master of movie extravaganza and Swanson as a leading lady of imperious beauty. Iribé's triumph would have wide influence on the future of motion picture set and costume design. "Give it *art!*" became a new studio command, as expanding budgets made more costly backgrounds and wardrobes possible. Henceforth, anything that hinted of European design was a badge of prestige.

De Mille would continue to use feathers in his productions' costumes into the late forties, when Edith Head gave Hedy Lamarr a cape of the plumage in Paramount's *Samson and Delilah.* De Mille had a penchant for peacock feathers and kept a flock of the birds in the gardens of his vast estate. A standard Hollywood joke was that "no peacock is safe around De Mille."

Iribe, a former assistant of Poiret's, was a major figure in the renaissance of French decorative art in the twenties. He designed almost every kind of item, from fabrics and jewelry to furniture, interiors, and crystal. There was hardly an artistic field on which Iribe did not put his distinctive stamp of decoration. A stylized rose became his logo, a trademark that would become a recurring design element for almost three decades.

Although Iribe's initial stay in Hollywood was brief, he returned there to design for De Mille's *The Affairs of Anatol* (1920), *The Ten Commandments* (1923), *The Road to Yesterday* (1925), and *Madam Satan* (1930), for which he created the décor and Adrian the costumes. *The Affairs of Anatol,* based on Arthur Schnitzler's play, is considered by many to be De Mille's most gorgeous production. Alvin Wyckoff's photography superbly illuminated Iribe's elegant sets, and the star, again, was Gloria Swanson, now widely heralded as "Glorious Gloria" by Paramount's publicity department. Claire West served as costume supervisor. Art as well as cinema critics praised the dazzling film, and immediately Hollywood's major studios began a search for design talents in theater and fashion centers abroad.

In 1920, William Randolph Hearst formed a motion picture company called Cosmopolitan Films to produce movies (which MGM would release) starring his adored Marion Davies. He brought Joseph Urban, former designer for Vienna's Burgtheater and the Ziegfeld Follies in New York, to California to serve as art director. MGM followed by luring Erté, the fashionable French designer, to Hollywood to create costumes for its top stars. Erté (who took his name from the French pronunciation of the initials of his real name, Romain de Tirtoff), a Russian and former assistant to Poiret, had already gained a considerable reputation in Europe. His stay in Hollywood was brief, however. After creating the costumes for an elaborate *bal des arts* sequence in *Restless Sex* (1920), starring Miss Davies, Erté returned to France.

Four years later, Louis B. Mayer sent for Erté to design the sets and costumes

The French artist-designer Paul Iribe acted as art director for Cecil B. De Mille's 1919 production Male and Female, with Gloria Swanson as its star. Claire West served as the film's costume designer-supervisor, but Iribe himself dressed Miss Swanson, shown here in the flashback sequence in which she appears as a Babylonian princess. Her intricate pearl costume and peacock headdress have rarely been equaled for sheer Hollywood magnificence, and Iribe's artistry brought the art of film costuming to new levels of the fantastic.

Another gown from Male and Female. This film exploited Swanson's haughty sophistication and style that would bring her fame, fortune, and, in 1925, a title, as wife of the Marquis de la Falaise.

PAUL
IRIBE

This stylized rose became the trademark of artist-designer Paul Iribe, and a symbol of French fashion and elegance during the twenties and thirties. It appeared embroidered on Poiret gowns, as a decoration for furniture, as lamp globes, and in jewelry. In 1926 the famed jeweler Cartier is said to have sold more than four hundred gold face-powder cases bearing enameled and jeweled versions of Iribe's design.

Cecil B. De Mille was so fond of peacock feathers that costumes for his productions continued to feature them. Here Hedy Lamaar, starring in Samson and Delilah (Paramount, 1949), appears in a cape created by Edith Head with feathers De Mille plucked from his own peacocks.

Ex-Follies girl Marion Davies was the first actress to be the raison d'être of a film. In fact, for her alone William Randolph Hearst started a production company in 1920, and flew designer Joseph Urban in from New York. Here Miss Davies appears in a costume for Paramount's When Knighthood Was in Flower *(1922)*.

French designer Erté in his studio at Sèvres in 1924. Louis B. Mayer's representative, who visited Erté there, was so impressed by its décor that he had photographers snap the room from every angle. When Erté later arrived in Culver City, he was astonished to find his studio re-created in every detail. Of Erté's arrival in America on February 25, 1925, The Morning Telegraph noted that his "advent into motion pictures is of special significance to the film industry as it is the first notable recognition paid to the importance of the costuming phase in motion picture production." (Photo courtesy Sevenarts Ltd. London)

Left: Gloria Swanson in Paramount's 1922 production of Her Gilded Cage, *the tale of a cabaret star who longs for the simple life. Miss Swanson's lampshade-skirted above-the-knee transparent dance dress of paillette-embroidered chiffon was wired at the hem for a conical shape. It epitomized a new kind of fashion daring, and only Swanson could wear it with such charm and authority.*

Above: During 1925, Erté created this costume for Gwen Lee in MGM's production of Bright Lights.

Right: Gloria Swanson in a gown from My American Wife *(Paramount, 1923).*

John Gilbert and Lillian Gish in MGM's production of La Bo-hème *(1926). Miss Gish, cast as the pathetic heroine, Mimi, rejected most of Erté's designs for her role. With the help of MGM's wardrobe mistress, she designed and made her own dresses.*

Clara Bow found her way into films by winning a beauty contest, but attracted only mild attention until the distinguée Elinor Glyn made her the "It" girl. This publicity portrait released by Paramount showed the pert, sadly vulnerable but altogether exquisite Miss Bow at her best. She epitomized the new young woman of the twenties: the good-natured working girl who climbs from slum life, marries her boss, and lives in a penthouse. She was the girl who couldn't lose. But in real life, little Clara faded fast—a few glorious years of fame (1925–29) and it was over. With her went the flapper, and the sleek sophisticate of the thirties stepped before the camera.

for several films at MGM. The designer was given the full Hollywood treatment: Without Erté's knowing it, Mayer arranged to have the designer's studio in France photographed in the most minute detail and reproduced by the studio's scenic department on the MGM lot. He was immediately provided with a chauffeured limousine, two French-speaking secretaries, and a luxurious bungalow at the Beverly Hills Hotel. To make sure this largess was not lost on the public, MGM's publicity hounds rounded up 197 interviews for Erté during his one-year stay. Newspapers and magazines across America carried columns devoted to the eccentric French visitor, with predictions of the lavish spectacles he would bring to celluloid reality.

Mae Murray, once a New York cabaret singer, was one of Hollywood's top stars when she appeared in MGM's 1925 film of Franz Lehar's storybook musical romance The Merry Widow. *Her frizzed hair, bee-stung lips, and heavily lined eyes, enhanced by Adrian's sophisticated costumes, made her the rage of the day.*

Clara Bow in her unsuccessful comeback, the Fox production Hoopla *(1933). Rita Kaufman designed this revealing outfit for Bow as a carnival cooch dancer.*

Settling into a hilltop house on Beechwood Drive in Hollywood, Erté made an earnest attempt to fulfill Mayer's great expectations of him. During 1925 he costumed *Monte Carlo,* a gown for Gwen Lee in *Bright Lights,* Aileen Pringle's wardrobe for *The Mystic,* and the clothes for *Dance Madness.* He also dressed the principals in King Vidor's production of *La Bohème,* a sad romance of the 1840s set in the Latin Quarter of Paris. Lillian Gish was cast as the pathetic heroine Mimi, John Gilbert played the poet Rodolfo, and the French actress Renée Adorée was given the role of Mimi's friend Musetta. A storm burst when Miss Gish rejected most of Erté's designs, firmly announcing that she would not wear them. Vidor made futile attempts to reconcile his star and the enraged designer, but Gish settled the matter by designing and, with the help of MGM wardrobe-mistress Lucia Coulter, making her own dresses.

Although his creations were charming and full of fantasy, Erté was unable to function under the constant pressure of working in Hollywood. Within a year, after designing costumes—which were never used—for a film entitled *Paris,* he announced he was forsaking American films forever; and in a flurry of publicity (during which he made several highly charged statements about the inadequacies of Hollywood movie production), he boarded a train for New York with his secretary and a mountain of luggage.

Erté left America in 1926, at the peak of the period F. Scott Fitzgerald has described as "the biggest, gaudiest spree in history," the Jazz Age. Movies had become part of American life; all over the country, women copied the fashions, hairstyles, makeup, and idiosyncracies of the stars. Flappers Charlestoned in beaded shifts like the ones worn by Joan Crawford and Nancy Carroll; Mae Murray's bee-stung lips (created by Max Factor) and her black lacquered fingernails started a vogue. When Bebe Daniels attributed her beautiful complexion to a facial mask composed of oatmeal, buttermilk, and honey, husbands everywhere arrived home after a day's work to be greeted by their wives with masks of sticky mush.

In their quest for beauty, women shingled their hair and emulated an air of abandon in the manner of Clara Bow, the ultimate flapper and new screen favorite who cast aside pre–World War I standards of behavior and exemplified the carefree. Cast in the role of a Charleston baby with a heart-of-gold vulnerability and an "anything you say, kid" good nature, Bow zoomed to stardom. In 1925 alone, she made fourteen movies. Inundated by twenty thousand fan letters a week, and tortured by insecurity from her sudden fame, she covered her fears with a hard gloss composed of a volatile temperament, self-indulgence, and a refusal to conform. But by 1930 her stardom had faded, and she retired from the screen. Three years later she tried a comeback with the unsuccessful *Hoopla,* made for Fox. This time Bow appeared as a carnival cooch dancer, costumed by Rita Kaufman. But the Jazz Age was over. . . . Bow became a recluse and was hospitalized for long periods in mental sanitariums. After several more unfortunate attempts to recapture her popularity, she lived in comparative obscurity until her death in 1965.

Hollywood itself underwent great changes in the twenties. More and more it began to assume the look of surreal elegance that, by the thirties, would set it apart from any other community in the world as the capital of the beautiful and the rich. Studio directors and executives lived in bougainvillea-covered pseudo-Spanish and -Tudor mansions with "California-style" interiors that boasted wrought-iron grillwork, tile floors, carved-beam ceilings, and brocade-upholstered Italian Renaissance furniture. On the rooftops of some houses (Tom Mix's, for one) the monograms of their star-residents sparkled at night with hundreds of tiny electric light bulbs.

Hollywood parties became larger and more boisterous; it was not at all unusual for 150 guests to assemble at the estate of Cecil B. De Mille or at the Douglas Fairbanks' hilltop château Pickfair for a Saturday night affair. On Friday night, the "in" crowd could be seen at the prizefights in Los Angeles, the actresses wrapped in chinchilla and ermine coats. ("Going to the fights was the

Off screen, the Fairbanks—America's "royalty"—visited the ruins of ancient Egypt. Mary wore a superb leopard coat over jodhpurs and jacket tailored on London's Savile Row by the same house that made Douglas's classic double-breasted polo coat.

Rather than the bouffant "waltz" gowns generally associated with the Merry Widow, Adrian put Murray in narrow, sleek, cleverly cut gowns that complemented the star's daring personality. Her waltz in the arms of the handsome John Gilbert was a slow, sensuous glide rather than the swirling ballroom exercise that had prevailed (and still does). Adrian's soigné designs contributed immensely to the success of Murray's tour de force.

only *other* thing to do in those days," Mae West remembers.) At the popular Montmartre Café, women danced in gowns often borrowed for the evening from a studio wardrobe department. Silk stockings decorated with clocks of lace embroidered with bugle beads, which often cost over a hundred dollars a pair, were de rigueur. During those early years, the life of a movie star was nonstop glory; everything was too new for anyone yet to be a has-been.

By 1925, fashion had become absolutely essential to movies. Gloria Swanson, Mae Murray, Ruth Chatterton, Constance Bennett, and Pola Negri were famous for both their screen clothes and their personal wardrobes. Studio designers were given enormous budgets to dress the stars, and films costing $1.5 million to produce were not unusual. Studio moguls like Zukor and Mayer were aware that it was good business to dress their stars like the fantastic creatures the public believed them to be, and they advertised their extravagance for all it was worth. Like treasures from an Eastern potentate, stacks of crates in studio workrooms brimming with silk velvets, chiffons, metallic lamés, and tons of beads, sequins, and paste jewels (for special stars, real jewels were not out of the question) were available to designers.

One of the most unique movie goddesses of the twenties was Mae Murray, and her most sensational role was in *The Merry Widow,* directed by Erich Von Stroheim for MGM in 1925. Gowned in a diamanté sheath of black satin, wearing a diamond-studded bandeau and clasping rare plumage, Miss Murray, her face powdered flat white, eyes heavily lined, and lips painted into a tiny heart, whirled spectacularly through the famous waltz in the arms of John Gilbert. Here was a new height of elegant romance, and the musical accompaniment (as for most movies until the advent of sound) was provided by a full orchestra in the larger movie palaces, a piano or organ in more modest movie houses. Murray's soigné beauty brought droves of people to the box office and established her as a symbol of twenties irresistibility.

The Merry Widow also brought the designer Adrian to public attention. It was his first major film assignment and it demonstrated his innate understanding of the relationship between photography and costume. When asked later how he had acquired his knowledge of the camera's eye, Adrian was at a loss for words. But he understood a principle that many movie designers rarely grasped: that fashion and fashion for *films* are totally different. His mastery of the technical difficulties faced by a movie designer set a standard of movie costuming that remains a model of excellence.

Adrian recognized that in movies the face of an actor is all-important. The camera seeks it out like a telescope, bringing the viewer closer and closer. Like an indiscreet eye, the camera prowls around examining attitudes, gestures, and emotions, sparing no detail. Thus, the clothes that frame the body must embellish the character in a way that asserts his or her personality. As in the theater, costumes serve to project a performer's role on the screen. Take away Charlie Chaplin's battered bowler hat and baggy pants, and you remove one of the major elements of his unforgettable film image.

While techniques of dressing for the camera were being refined, an innovation that would eliminate the need for the mighty Wurlitzers accompanying silent films in movie halls across the land was being developed. When Al Jolson got down on one knee to sing "Mammy" in *The Jazz Singer* (1927), the first talking picture, a new era in Hollywood began.

3

1927-1939

THE CLASSIC ERA

THE ERRATIC YEARS BETWEEN THE END OF WORLD WAR I AND "BLACK FRI-day," when the stock market began its collapse, ended—and with them went the vamps, flappers, Latin lovers, "Our Gang," Rin Tin Tin, and the silents. Despite the Great Depression, Hollywood fashion, production, and society flowered in the mid-thirties. It was a time when bias-cut crêpe de Chine gowns and satin pumps were worn for dancing to the wistful tunes of Cole Porter.

By then, the creation of a star had become routine. A star was not born, but made. Hair was bleached or dyed, and, if necessary, to "open" the eyes, eyebrows were removed and penciled in above the natural line. Studio-resident dentists, expert at creating million-dollar smiles, capped teeth or fitted them with braces. Cosmetic surgery was often advised to reshape the nose of a new recruit or tighten her sagging chin. A "starlet" was taught how to walk, smile, laugh, and weep. She was instructed in the special techniques of acting before a camera, perfecting pronunciation, and learning how to breathe for more effective voice control. Days were spent in wardrobe, situated in separate buildings within the studio communities.

By 1930, wardrobe departments of major studios had grown to be small factories that employed as many as two hundred workers, and throughout the thirties they churned out costumes by the hundreds. Pattern makers, fitters, seamstresses, tailors, milliners, furriers, embroiderers, and even armorers and jewelers were employed.

The structure of a movie wardrobe department, as originally set up to supply Griffith and De Mille with the vast number of costumes they demanded, closely followed that of a Broadway costume shop. Clothes were turned out in assembly-line fashion. Once a muslin pattern was perfected, cutters shaped the cloth, seamstresses basted it together, and fitters worked on it—first on dress dummies, and then fitting it to the actress's body; the designer personally often did the final fittings. As they grew in size these departments also became stratified, each with a chief designer, head of wardrobe, several junior designers, sketchers, and period researchers. Always, a trusted and indispensable *vendeuse* stood at the designer's right hand, a combination assistant, girl Friday, and troubleshooter.

Western Costume, Hollywood's largest costume rental company (it is still thriving), could be depended on to provide the wardrobe for the large groups of extras often required in a production, but the garments for leading actors and principals were created for them alone and executed with painstaking care. When a picture was completed, its costumes were hung on racks in wardrobe storerooms, later to be used for extras or remodeled for supporting players. Thousands of costumes accumulated, and by the thirties vast amounts of apparel were available for "fill in" for a production, generally selected by an assistant designer.

Resident studio designers were provided with well-appointed working quarters located in the costume-department building, decorated to the individual's liking at company expense. At MGM, Adrian, who was gifted with a flair for interior decoration, frequently changed the décor of his offices during his seventeen-year tenure. An ardent collector of antique furniture and objets d'art, his elegant inner sanctum became the envy of other studio designers, who strove to outdo him. When Jack Warner stormed over Orry-Kelly's plan to cover his reception room's ceiling with gold leaf, Kelly compromised by substituting silver leaf. However, his attempts to have a small bar installed on the premises were met with an unequivocal veto. Undaunted, Kelly bought a bar with casters that could be rolled out of sight when word reached him that Warner was about to pay a visit.

Travis Banton's rooms in the wardrobe building at Paramount were painted and carpeted in greige, a neutral color between gray and beige that enhanced his eclectic selection of period and modern furniture, crystal wall sconces, and contemporary French paintings. With multiview mirrors, satin-covered banquettes, and padded and carpeted fitting platforms, his quarters rivaled those found in the hushed atmosphere of Parisian salons.

Chief designers were responsible for dressing both star actors and actresses in a film, but some, like Adrian, preferred to dress only women, and would delegate the men's costumes, as well as clothes for minor roles, to his assistants. As a result, some assistants costumed only male actors. Top male stars had their clothes tailored for them from sketches, as did leading female stars. Giles Steele

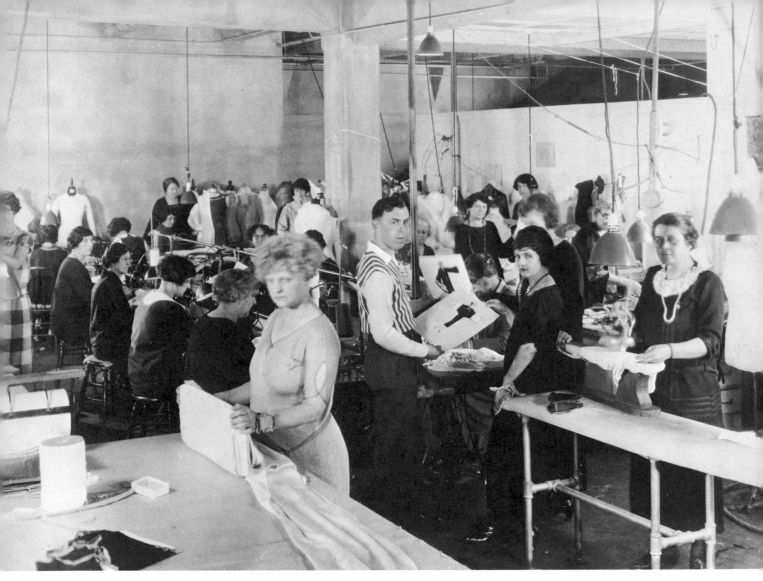

Designer Howard Greer in the workroom at Paramount.

at MGM would be credited on screen for his contribution to a film. He was responsible for a number of trends in men's clothing. The casual look of Cary Grant and the elegance of Fred Astaire's impeccably cut clothes made their mark on male fashion in America. Ensembles for supporting players were taken on completely by the chief designer's assistants, or by junior designers, and their sketches had to receive the approval of both the head designer and the director.

Another responsibility of a head designer's assistant was the preparation of a detailed wardrobe plot, showing precisely the sequence of ensembles a star was to wear in the scenes shot. Each scene was numbered, and in the plot a brief note was made as to which costume would be needed for each particular scene. The accuracy of such a directive was vital to the progress of a film and it was nicknamed "the Bible." Deviating from the plan and having the wrong costume

Travis Banton's first assignment as a movie costume designer for Paramount was The Dress-maker from Paris *(1925). Here he checks a costume on the set.*

ready for a scene would cause expensive delays, and the wrath of the producer and the director would descend upon the designer.

Each designer had his particular manner of working. Adrian, for example, first did a rough sketch of his idea, then draped the actual fabric he was using for the design on a dress dummy, padded to duplicate the star's dimensions. When he was satisfied with the results, he would sketch the gown and present it for approval. Banton, on the other hand, relied solely on his own sketches. When one was approved, he turned it over to drapers to create a muslin pattern on the star's personal dress form.

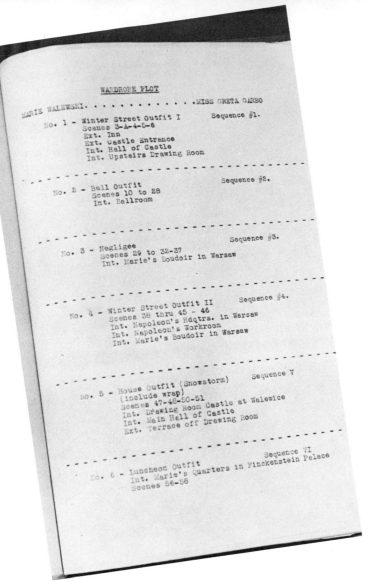

WARDROBE PLOT

MARIE WALEWSKI. . . . . .MISS GRETA GARBO

No. 1 – Winter Street Outfit I   Sequence #1.
     Scenes 3-A-4-5-6
     Ext. Inn
     Ext. Castle Entrance
     Int. Hall of Castle
     Int. Upstairs Drawing Room

No. 2 – Ball Outfit   Sequence #2.
     Scenes 10 to 28
     Int. Ballroom

No. 3 – Negligee   Sequence #3.
     Scenes 29 to 32-37
     Int. Marie's Boudoir in Warsaw

No. 4 – Winter Street Outfit II   Sequence #4.
     Scenes 38 thru 45 – 46
     Int. Napoleon's Hdqtrs. in Warsaw
     Int. Napoleon's Workroom
     Int. Marie's Boudoir in Warsaw

No. 5 – House Outfit (Snowstorm)   Sequence V
     (include wrap)
     Scenes 47-48-50-51
     Int. Drawing Room Castle at Walewice
     Int. Main Hall of Castle
     Ext. Terrace off Drawing Room

No. 6 – Luncheon Outfit   Sequence VI
     Int. Marie's Quarters in Finckenstein Palace
     Scenes 56-58

A page of the wardrobe plot for Garbo as Marie Walewski in MGM's 1937 production of Conquest, *in which Charles Boyer played Napoleon and Garbo was his Polish mistress. Each sequence lists a scene or number of scenes indicating which costume Garbo was to wear and the locations where it would be used. Sequence No. 2, for instance, notes that the actress would wear a ball gown in Scenes 10 to 28. Known as the wardrobe department's "Bible," the plan had to be strictly adhered to. Though Adrian did his usual superb job in costuming his favorite star, Garbo's particular charms were not best suited to the Empire period in which the drama was set.*

Normally a designer's sketches were returned to his or her desk as quickly as possible to enable work on the costume to proceed. Often, a complete model of the new design was made up in a relatively inexpensive fabric that approximated the final materials to be used. Sometimes duplicate costumes were made, particularly if a gown was to receive an unusual amount of stress—worn in a simulated rain storm, splattered with some substance, etc. Also, duplicates were often insurance against delays in shooting; if a star spilled a drop of coffee on her gown while resting between takes, it would be impossible to proceed without first cleaning the gown, a time-consuming and thus costly effort. Instead, the duplicate costume could be called for and the shooting schedule maintained. A duplicate costume could also serve when publicity photos were needed for promotion. In the instance of Mae West, two versions of the same gown were usually made: one in which Miss West stood or walked, and one for the rare occasions when she would sit (more often recline) on a couch or chair. The gowns made for her when standing were fitted so tightly the actress found it impossible to assume any kind of sitting position without bursting her seams!

Mae West reclining in a gown by Travis Banton.

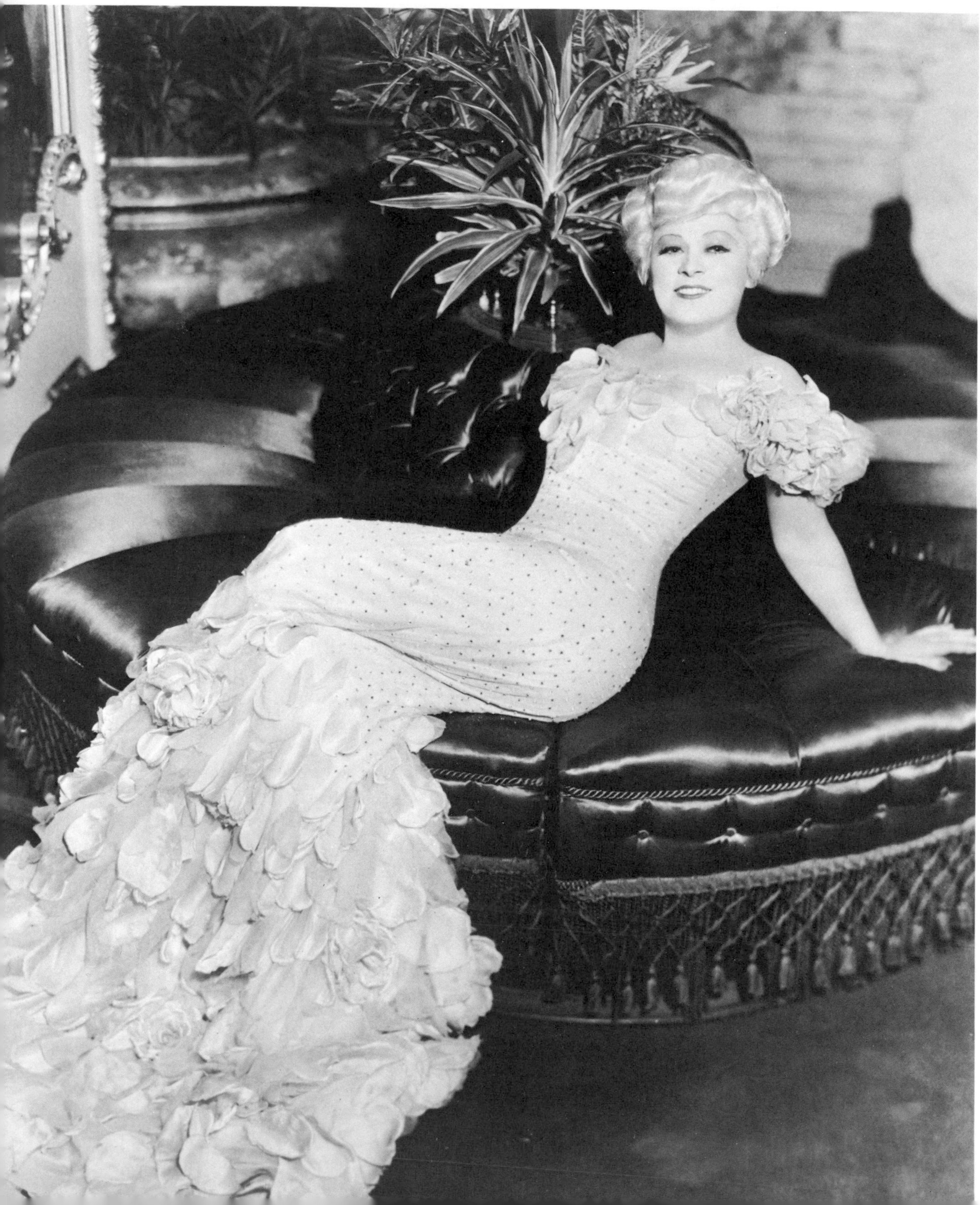

Rarely was an actress blessed with a mannequin's figure. It was the designer's responsibility to create an illusion of physical perfection, concealing defects and stressing good points. Special undergarments were often made to achieve a sylphlike silhouette, but if a designer felt it necessary, he recommended the imperfect beauty be launched on a program of diet, exercise, and massage. Daily visits to the studio gym would be scheduled for the actress, and a nutritionist would be consulted. In extreme cases, a doctor would prescribe medications to assist the actress in slimming down. In the case of Judy Garland, such a practice laid the foundation for tragedy.

For new contract actresses, a studio's expert drapers armed with muslin, pins, and scissors worked to find the style of neckline, bodice, sleeve, and skirt that was most flattering. Wearing a perfectly fitted basic garment of muslin, the actress was then photographed from every angle, and the prints were studied by the designer, who decided whether a special type of foundation garment was necessary to enhance her figure. The photographs were then filed and referred to when she was to have a new wardrobe for a film. "They were like those pictures they take of criminals before they send them to prison," Betty Grable once recalled; "all our measurements, with our names written under them." Then a dress form was padded and a kapok-stuffed facsimile of the star's arm was added to the dummy. Each dummy was labeled with the name of the star, or star-to-be, and joined all the others that lined the workrooms.

Fittings, each of which might last two to six hours, were the bane of a star's life. An actress often spent more time in front of a mirror, as workers scurried about her snipping and pinning and adjusting a new costume, than she did before a camera. A star of the magnitude of Dietrich, Crawford, or Garbo could have as many as twenty costumes for a film, and each could require three, four, and sometimes as many as six fittings. Every wardrobe department contained a private room with a small bed where an exhausted actress could rest before continuing with the arduous ordeal. At Paramount, Carole Lombard often took catnaps between fittings, and on occasion her snoring could be heard in the adjoining workrooms.

Finished costumes were viewed in the blinding glare of spotlights that approximated the harsh illumination they would receive on the set. The designer, with his or her assistants, examined each garment minutely and corrected telltale mistakes that would be magnified countless times on the screen. A forgotten basting thread or an off-center buttonhole which would ordinarily go unnoticed could cause calamity in a closeup.

It was not unusual for six or eight beaders to labor for several weeks, painstakingly covering delicate silk chiffon or crêpe with minuscule bugle beads for a gown that might appear for no more than a minute in the edited film: Often the scene in which such a costly garment was worn ended up being cut from the film entirely. Sometimes such discarded costumes could be used in another film made by the original actress, but more often they were put in the stock room, where clothes went after filming. Claudette Colbert recalled often seeing one of her beautiful Banton dresses from an earlier film on an extra in a later picture.

Carole Lombard was a devoted client of Travis Banton, and he designed for her both on and off the screen. This 1934 Paramount photo shows them selecting exquisite, exclusive materials for her gowns in Rumba.

Workers in Paramount's wardrobe department painstakingly apply beads to a glamorous pink evening gown designed by Banton for Carole Lombard in The Princess Comes Across (1936).

Finished costumes were guarded like treasures until the moment they were to be used before the cameras. Once dressed, a star was attended by her personal dressers and maid, as well as several wardrobe workers whose job it was to see that the precious garment was protected from soil and damage. Wrinkles in the fabric became a matter of great concern; to prevent them, the "leaning board" was invented. A padded wooden plank, much like an extended ironing board, was equipped with armrests and placed on supports at a ninety-degree angle. This contrivance, which included a footrest at the bottom, allowed an actress to relax in a leaning position with some semblance of comfort between takes—without wrinkling her gown.

Happily, some of the most extravagant costumes made for movies have survived. The crew at Paramount, for example, guarded a precious cache of priceless beaded dresses that Travis Banton designed for the studio's top stars during the thirties. Among them is a two-piece chiffon dinner gown solidly covered with a paisley design worked in gold bugle beads accented with paste rubies, emeralds, topazes, and diamonds, together with a matching sable-banded stole. The ensemble was worn by Marlene Dietrich in *Angel* (1937), the last film for which the actress and Banton worked together. Requiring weeks of work, the costume was cost-listed at eight thousand dollars on the wardrobe records (it would cost at least six times as much to make today). Even more remarkable is the fact that it was only one of several such gowns in the film that were seen only fleetingly.

Sound movies brought added problems to movie costumers. Particular fabrics were discovered to be impossible to use; the rustle of taffeta and certain satins was picked up by a sensitive microphone and, in Adrian's words, magnified to sound "like an approaching army truck." Jewelry, too, had to be carefully chosen, or the clanking of heavy earrings might drown out the words of love whispered by a star to her leading man in a close-up. A squeaking shoe could mean that production on a film had to be suspended until the offending sound was eliminated. Actresses were cautioned not to tap their long fingernails on a table-top or cigarette box, and the clasp on a hand bag had to be sent off to the prop department to be made soundless with bits of tape or felt before it was used.

The painstaking production of a film's costumes could cause delays in shooting, but confrontations over costume sometimes jeopardized schedules, too. There are many classic stories of designer-actress feuds that, in retrospect, sound more amusing than they were at the time. As with all folklore, it is difficult to know where fact ends and invention begins, but some of the tales of workroom feuds make for amusing telling. It is said that once Travis Banton looked out of his office window in Paramount's costume department (near the studio's main gate) to observe the approach of the fiery Nancy Carroll, arriving for a fitting. He moaned to an assistant, "Here comes my cross!" Some weeks earlier at a fitting, Miss Carroll had indicated her displeasure with an elaborate beaded gown Banton had designed for her, by silently tearing his creation off her body in shreds and walking out without a word. Banton never forgave her act of quiet rage and turned her over to his assistant Edith Head as soon as he could.

Jean Harlow, resting on a leaning board between takes for Dinner at Eight *(MGM, 1933).*

Marlene Dietrich, flanked by Herbert Marshall at her right and Melvyn Douglas at her left, is wearing a Fabergé-inspired creation that Travis Banton designed for Paramount's 1937 Angel. *A stole of the same beaded chiffon edged with thick bands of Russian sable added the final touch of luxe to this superb and costly garment.*

Explaining his action to Zukor, the enraged designer claimed the actress had gotten so plump that he could no longer dress her. Consequently, "Papa" Zukor ordered Carroll to go on a near-starvation diet.

A less-often-told nugget of gossip suggests that a conflict developed between Banton and Claudette Colbert, ordinarily one of his staunchest supporters, over the costumes he designed for her in De Mille's costly Egyptian fantasy *Cleopatra* (1934). Although the modern clothes he had created for the actress to wear both on and off the screen had met with her enthusiastic approval, his sketches of her gowns for this movie aroused her to heights of rage she rarely displayed. Patient at first, Banton redesigned her costumes, but his second set of sketches was returned scrawled with her very frank opinion that they were unflattering, vulgar conceptions. Accustomed to being treated with the greatest respect and having his designs accepted without question, he found Miss Colbert's second rejection unbearable. Furious, he strode across the lot to the star's dressing room to vent his anger, and anyone within the confines of the Paramount community could have heard the heated insults the two exchanged. Finally, Banton shouted he would send one more set of designs to Miss Colbert; if *they* did not meet her requirements, he suggested she cut her wrists, for he would not paint any further sketches.

By the time Banton had returned to his office, word of the emotional scene with Miss Colbert had reached his staff, who were waiting tensely for the next act in the melodrama to unfold. Without a word, the shaken designer went directly to his private office and locked himself in. It was almost midnight before he reappeared and wearily tossed a new set of sketches onto a table, instructing an assistant to see that they were delivered to the actress first thing the next morning. Then he announced his need for a few drinks and drove off in his pale green Packard roadster.

The following day, Banton nervously awaited the star's reaction to his new designs. It was late afternoon before a messenger returned with them. Banton quickly opened the portfolio, shrieked, and held up the drawings to his staff as he cursed the actress. The beautifully painted sketches were stained with what was obviously dried blood!

Only later did Banton learn that Miss Colbert, still not pleased with his conception of her as the Queen of the Nile, had deliberately cut her finger on a sharp edge of the thick paper they were painted on and smeared them with her blood. Banton fled the studio again, this time to Palm Springs. Three days later, a phone call from "Papa" himself, assuring the wounded designer that everything had been worked out with "The Colbert" satisfactorily, brought Banton back to the studio, heavy-eyed and still unsteady after what must have been many more than "a few."

Part of the initiation of a movie actress involved learning how to project "star quality," a kind of ever-warm but slightly aloof benevolence when seen socially or at public functions. Teachers of "charm" were hired by the studios to instruct fledglings in this art, a custom that began in the twenties when Elinor Glyn

Of the numerous films that portray the life and loves of Egypt's Cleopatra, perhaps none was as visually extraordinary as that produced and directed by Cecil B. De Mille for Paramount in 1934. As the "Serpent of the Nile," Claudette Colbert wore a series of extraordinary pseudo-Egyptian operettalike costumes created for her by Travis Banton. Her small figure draped and bandaged in shimmering lamé, Colbert made a Cleopatra no Antony could possibly have resisted.

reigned as a kind of social arbiter in Hollywood. The sister of the internationally known couturière Lucile, Glyn's sensational novella *Three Weeks,* which told of a fictitious Balkan princess who spends three weeks with a young British aristocrat in a luxurious chalet in Switzerland, brought her fame.

Immediately upon her arrival in Hollywood, Miss Glyn established herself as knowing everything right about everything: which fork to use, how to sip wine, how to use a fan at dinner, how to nod regally at a mob of screaming fans. Gloria Swanson was one of the impressive Miss Glyn's protégées and Glyn claimed to have taught the rising star how to behave with the éclat for which she would later be known. Miss Glyn brought a kind of "haute chic" to Hollywood; for all matters concerned with style and class, hers was believed to be the last word.

As part of the training program for stardom, a hopeful was suddenly confronted by countless other new and awesome responsibilities. The training was grueling and sometimes cruel, but the newcomer endured her ordeal without complaint. The stakes were high, and it was the chance of a lifetime. Completing the obstacle course generally took up to six months, but the tension and discomfort of those days dissolved when she stood for the first time in front of the cameras and the watchful eyes of studio executives, directors, cameramen, production assistants, makeup artists, hairdressers, and crew.

If she made it to the top, as a star she was assured one of the simple but luxurious dressing rooms in her studio's special building devoted to stars' quarters. "Dream stables," some called them, long rows of smallish suites equipped with commodious dressing tables, a comfortable chair or two, a chaise longue upon which an actress might rest, and a full tiled bathroom. For the very important stars a reception room was provided as well; there the actress might meet with members of the press or eat her lunch in a degree of privacy and style.

The new contract actress also learned very soon that she was committed to whatever the front office deemed best for her as part of a multimillion-dollar business empire. Depending on the terms she had accepted, her life thenceforth would be controlled by the studio for two to seven years. Studio heads held absolute power and authority over thousands of employees, and each one presided over his domain like a benevolent but firm father-chieftain who demanded absolute devotion and obedience from his family. Feared and often hated by the stars whose lives and careers they dominated, the movie moguls also insisted on a strict moral code. Scandal was deadly. The censoring arm of the feared Hays Office dictated how long a kiss might last on the screen and, even worse, how much cleavage a costume designer could allow an actress to reveal. There were rules concerning attitudes of posture (a man and woman lying in bed together was forbidden), language (Rhett Butler's famed "Frankly, my dear, I don't give a damn," in 1939, aroused a storm of controversy within the studio), and how many cocktails a movie's "decent" character could be seen to drink on the screen. In addition, a star's private life was scrutinized by the studio publicity department, which feared that the discovery of an indiscretion would send Hedda Hopper or Louella Parsons rushing to her typewriter with shrieks of joy.

Privacy was something a star had to give up as a price for fame. "You can't even show a baby's bare behind out here," Jean Harlow once roared, when warned her bias-cut Adrian gowns clung to her too revealingly.

Wearing the royal approval of William Randolph Hearst like an impregnable suit of armor, Louella Parsons, oracle of Hollywood, possessed the power to break the careers of those in movies who had the misfortune to incur her (or Hearst's) disapproval. Miss Parsons kept a card catalogue of Hollywood personalities and, it is said, on rainy afternoons would thumb through it to recall a slight or an imagined insult some poor soul had paid her. The punishment for a slight to "Lollypops" could be devastating. Adrian, for example, once neglected to offer her what she considered proper homage at a party given for Marion Davies, and the following day she wondered in her column if perhaps his designs for "dear Joan Crawford" were becoming unflattering. Her words resulted in a hastily summoned meeting with MGM's head of production, Irving Thalberg, who instructed that henceforth the designer was to obtain his personal approval for all sketches of Miss Crawford's costumes.

Louella's rival, Hedda Hopper, could be difficult, too, though she never embarked on a vendetta against a costume designer. Adrian and Hedda were good friends; the designer found her amusing and enjoyed having her at his small dinner parties. He also was generous to the never-too-well-off actress-columnist and would pass on to her odds and ends of apparel that had been discarded from a film. Hedda herself would alter the leftovers and wear them about town, pointing out her new Adrian ensemble at the drop of one of her over-garnished hats. When it came to a star's morals or political beliefs, however, Hopper could eject venom like a cobra from her fountain pen. But it was her broad statements concerning a Hollywood notable that at last brought her to ruin when she wrote she knew a certain popular leading man was a homosexual. He sued her and eventually Hedda forfeited almost her entire fortune when the court's decision went against her. Hedda had tried, on occasion, to court the favor of Louella's employer, Hearst, but it was to no avail.

Though newspaper coverage was certainly important, it was the glossy movie magazines that were really responsible for the fabulous image of Hollywood during its heyday. The first such publication appeared in 1911 with the establishment of *Photoplay* by the Cloud Publishing Company in Chicago. But the real fan magazine—filled with never-less-than-sensational ballyhoo—reached its zenith during the thirties. *Silver Screen, Screen Book, Screenland, Modern Screen,* and *Motion Picture* (as well as *Photoplay*) indoctrinated their readers with the fantasy that in Hollywood all women were beautiful, crime did not pay, husbands and wives lived happily ever after, and that it was possible for anyone to become a movie star (if the real stars, above, were "right"). Provocative titles such as "The True Story of Garbo's Childhood," " 'I'm No Gigolo!' Says George Raft," "Shirley Temple's Letter to Santa Claus," and "Tarzan Seeks a Divorce" were accepted as gospel by unquestioning fans.

Feature articles about Beverly Hills' star-mansions carried exotic descriptions of swimming pools lined with blue mirrors (only one such actually existed), carpeted doggie kennels, bathrooms decorated to look like Roman bawdy houses, and gardens illuminated at night by hidden klieg moonlight where tame apes roamed at will. There was generally an Editor's Page with editorials, usually criticizing a star's behavior (" 'Behave Yourself, Clark!' " "Warning to Hollywood-bound Girls," " 'Watch Out, Ann Dvorak' "), a page that offered Favorite Recipes of the Stars ("Try Kay Francis' Pineapple and Avocado Omelette"), the inevitable Advice to Those in Love, and diagrams from which one might learn the latest Hollywood dance craze ("The Secret of Bonita Granville's Conga").

Always, too, there was a fashion page with photographs of stars wearing their latest film costumes and with tips on how to emulate their glamorous apparel ("Let Your Prom Dress Be Merle Oberon's *Wuthering Heights* Party Gown"). Makeup advice was included ("Paint and Powder Made Dietrich Beautiful"), and notes on etiquette ("Lupe Used the Wrong Fork!"). Photographs of actresses modeling their personal wardrobes were particularly popular, as were the elaborate creations they wore for premieres or important social events.

The word *fabulous* is defined by *The Oxford Universal Dictionary* as: "Of the nature of, or belonging to fable, full of fables, mythical, legendary, unhistorical . . . astonishing, incredible." This aptly describes the kind of tales movie magazines spun, and "fabulous" became Hollywood's own motto. By the thirties, the private lives of the stars had changed. Gone were the fake Spanish and Tudor houses of the twenties, replaced by white-pillared plantation- or Regency-style mansions decorated with French paintings, silver-leafed bamboo furniture, swagged chiffon curtains, and immense Lalique crystal bowls in which gardenias floated. Life's necessities embraced an intimate projection room, tennis courts, three-car garages, and (for the very rich) a completely equipped beauty salon with hair-dryer, massage table, steam cabinet, and gymnasium where a star could be "worked over" prior to a public appearance.

This affluence was accompanied by the raising of strict social barriers, and being a movie star did not in itself guarantee acceptance into the new society of movie élite led by Hearst and Marion Davies, the Irving Thalbergs, and the Basil Rathbones. Ouida Rathbone was a superb hostess; her parties at the Rathbones' Bel-Air estate were without equal. Such out-of-Hollywood-context guests as Artur Rubinstein, Somerset Maugham, Aldous Huxley, Lotte Lehmann, the Grand Duchess Marie of Russia, and (from the New York theater) Katharine Cornell made an invitation to dine at the Rathbones' one of the most sought-after engraved summonses in the movie colony. To have been seen at the Rathbones' assured entrée into the houses of Hollywood's inner circle. To be ignored meant either one had not yet "arrived," or, worse, was tinged with something akin to being déclassé.

Anything *British* was "in." "The British are coming!" Jack Warner once quipped. The core of the Rathbone "regulars" was the English colony that had migrated to Hollywood—a group of suave, elegantly speaking leading men who were the envy of American male stars. Errol Flynn, Ronald Colman, Clive Brook, Herbert Marshall, Laurence Olivier, Charles Chaplin, Cary Grant, and the distinguished C. Aubrey Smith were the most prominent. They formed their own social set, had Scottish governesses for their children and English cooks, drove to the studio in a Rolls-Royce or a Jaguar roadster, stopped working at four each afternoon for tea, and toasted their monarch's health when they gathered for a dinner party that featured a Mayfair menu. "You never saw so much roast beef and trifle in your life!" Ouida would later recall.

For one Christmas Eve party during the mid-thirties, the Rathbones decorated the grounds of their estate with the entire stock of several Christmas-tree suppliers. They had a team of studio scenic experts cover the trees with false snow, bathe them in pale blue spotlights, and then heap the driveway with a mixture of untoasted cornflakes and shredded paraffin to provide a running ground for a horse-drawn sleigh with bells, borrowed from a prop department. Finally (after making a generous contribution to a Beverly Hills Methodist church), they arranged to have a group of choir boys, their cheeks rouged to a traditional apple-rosiness and dressed in costumes Dolly Tree had designed for MGM's *David Copperfield,* wander about the grounds singing "God Rest Ye, Merry Gentlemen" and "Deck the Halls." Escorted by Noel Coward, Marlene Dietrich arrived for the party wearing an ensemble designed especially for the festivities by Travis Banton. It was later described by the press as consisting of "a Santa Claus–red velvet evening coat with white ermine collar and cuffs, worn over a draped white chiffon evening gown covered with tiny green bugle bead holly leaves with ruby-stone berries." After supper, Marlene was persuaded to sing "Stille Nacht" as two little "elves" (midgets hired for the evening from Central Casting) distributed gold-foil-wrapped gifts to the more than one-hundred guests. "What a sweet old-fashioned evening" it had been, Louella's column later rhapsodized.

By 1935 formal dinner parties had become Hollywood's main social diversion. Again, it was the Rathbones who set the style when they were the first in the film colony to request that full formal attire—gowns for the women and white tie and tails for the men—be worn at their gatherings. Hollywood's leading tailors enjoyed a deluge of orders for tail coats, and a number of studio designers, alert to a growing need, profited immensely by opening custom apparel salons where they presented three collections a year to a large and wealthy West Coast clientele. "We dressed to the teeth for everything," Ouida Rathbone later said. "It became a mania. Never the same gown twice, a hairdresser would come to the house the day of a party, and for especially important events a makeup man would come from the studio to do my face. Our clothes had a look quite unlike those from New York or Paris. I suppose you might call it a 'California' look. The evening dresses were quite spectacular." And so was Ouida's yearly bill from Adrian's Wilshire Boulevard salon (which first opened in 1942), with its shocking five-figure total. "Dear Basil always became so cross," she reminisced.

Besides Adrian, Howard Greer, Orry-Kelly, Travis Banton, Irene, and Vera West offered couture collections that gradually influenced the seasonal lines offered by New York manufacturers. More and more the look became the "Hollywood" look, exaggerated, daring, and highly original, an American projection into the once French-dominated world of international fashion.

The contribution Hollywood designers made to the image of the great stars is inestimable. If it is true that Garbo had "the face of the century" and that Dietrich was the "thirties' most exquisite creation," it also took professional artistry to transform a shy Swedish shopgirl into a glacially alluring creature who exuded mystery, and to turn a plump cabaret singer from postwar Berlin into "the orchid of Paramount."

Joan Crawford was Adrian's greatest challenge, with her bold mouth, wide glistening eyes, and stallion nostrils, and MGM's designer succeeded in meeting it brilliantly. One of Adrian's most famed creations for Miss Crawford was the gown made of layers of white organdy ruffles in *Letty Lynton* (1932). The dress started a rage of similar organdy confections on the screen and was widely copied by New York's Seventh Avenue (Macy's claimed to have sold fifty thousand inexpensive copies of Adrian's design). But it was the wide-shouldered, narrow-hipped silhouette that Adrian gave Crawford in the late thirties that became her most important fashion trademark. Designers who dressed the actress after Adrian's retirement continued to stress his basic formula. The forceful "Crawford look" became the ideal for millions of American women and turned up on models gliding through Paris salons. Thus, within two decades Hollywood was influencing rather than being influenced by Parisian designs.

It was also common for one designer's discovery of a style or form of decoration to be adapted by others. An example is the decorative motif of laurel leaves that at one time or another seems to have been spotlighted by almost every major costumer in Hollywood. Versions of the decoration were repeated countless times for movie costumes and, no doubt, will continue to be used to advantage as long as clothes are made specifically for film.

Adrian also applied his sense of flair and elegance to period costumes, establishing a kind of "period chic" that was a unique Hollywood innovation. For MGM's lavish *Marie Antoinette* (1938), Louis B. Mayer opened the coffers of his thriving studio to re-create the fabled court of Louis XVI, much to the delight of Adrian and art director Cedric Gibbons. The film took almost three years to make, and a staff of research experts spent months in Europe gathering antique prints, folios of drawings, actual garments of the period, and rare accessories. Possibly never before or since has so much research gone into the production of a period motion picture (unlike Poiret's approach to Bernhardt's *Elizabeth* in 1912)! Carefully packed, the costume material was shipped back to MGM, where Adrian meticulously studied it and then painted hundreds of sketches for his workrooms.

For the execution of Adrian's designs, special silk velvets and brocades were woven in Lyons, France's silk center, and hundreds of yards of gold and silver

Joan Crawford wearing the sensational ruffled gown Adrian gave her for MGM's 1932 success *Letty Lynton*. *Among the most famous costumes Adrian designed, the Lynton dress was copied commercially with tremendous success and made New York's Seventh Avenue acutely aware of the fact that Hollywood was a source for fashion exploitation that could out-sell Paris. Adrian's creations were particularly in tune with what the American woman wanted, and his wide-shouldered suits and daring style of decoration swept the country.*

Joan Crawford, costumed by Adrian for MGM's 1937 fashion-oriented Mannequin. To match Miss Crawford's intense screen personality, the designer gave her this no-nonsense broad-shouldered black wool suit lavished with gold and jewel-embroidered motifs. The immense hat and handbag, with a repeat of the decorative device, make for an arresting, highly original ensemble.

Designers often borrowed effective decorative motifs from each other. Pictured (above, left) is the laurel-leaf-adorned black gown Travis Banton first designed for Mae West. The ornamental detail was later adapted by Edith Head for Mary Martin (above) in Paramount's Rhythm on the River *(1940), and still another version of the motif highlights Lena Horne's costume (left) designed by Irene for the MGM picture* As Thousands Cheer *(1943).*

Norma Shearer starred in MGM's 1938 production of Marie Antoinette, *costumed in lavish period designs by Adrian.*

Gladys George as Mme Du Barry in Marie Antoinette. *Ouida Rathbone wore this dress to the famous costume ball given by Marion Davies in honor of William Randolph Hearst's seventy-fifth birthday.*

The detailed re-creation of the court of Louis XVI in Marie Antoinette *required extensive research and Adrian's elegant, imaginative designs.*

lace and intricate trimmings were imported from the few small factories in Austria and Italy that still manufactured them. Eight embroiderers were brought from Hungary to decorate the costumes with exquisite handwork, and a former milliner of the Imperial Russian Opera costume department, discovered in Paris, agreed to oversee the making of hundreds of hats and headdresses for the film. Sidney Guillaroff, MGM's famed hairdresser (whom Joan Crawford had discovered working in Antoine's salon at Saks Fifth Avenue in New York) made Norma Shearer's eighteen wigs, and Jack Dawn created her porcelainlike makeup. Dozens of copies of eighteenth-century buckled shoes were made by hand. Embroidered gloves and a fortune in jewelry, some set with genuine precious

stones and diamonds, were assembled. Not even history's real Marie Antoinette had been dressed with a more lavish hand!

Miss Shearer, a Canadian-born actress, also assumed a royal position on the set. As the wife of Irving Thalberg, MGM's head of production and Hollywood's *Wunderkind,* she reigned over the MGM lot. The thirty-four costumes Adrian designed for her as the doomed French queen are unsurpassed in magnificence, and a year before shooting began on the film, a separate storage building was constructed in the MGM compound to house them. The actress was so thrilled with her wardrobe that she gave Adrian a set of crystal goblets he had always admired in her home. Occasionally she arranged after-dinner visits with a party of friends to the storeroom, where she would model her lavish gowns for them.

But unfortunately Shearer's attainment of the role of Marie Antoinette and her eagerness to display her charms wearing Adrian's eighteenth-century confections led to a complete falling out between the Thalbergs and the man considered by many to be the most powerful in America at that time, William Randolph Hearst. A *cause célèbre* in the highest Hollywood tradition occurred when these two pillars of movie-colony society met head-on in a clash caused by Shearer's capriciousness and Adrian's gorgeous creations.

Hearst had long coveted for Marion Davies a number of the roles Thalberg had assigned to his wife. At that time Davies was a descending MGM luminary, and Hearst stoutly maintained that the re-creation of Marie Antoinette's short reign on film would restore his "little lady" to full star status. When Thalberg gave the part to Shearer, Hearst, unaccustomed to losing anything he wanted, moved his production company, his beloved star, and her fourteen-room dressing "bungalow" from MGM to the Warner Brothers Pasadena complex. Marion, however, who had always been a close friend of Norma's and who had pursued a career as a movie actress primarily to flatter Hearst's vanity, continued to see the Thalbergs socially, much to the displeasure of "W. R." She made a point of always including them on the guest list for the annual fancy-dress birthday party she gave for Hearst at the Beach House, a 110-room pseudo-Georgian villa he had built for her beside the ocean in Santa Monica.

In 1938, to commemorate Hearst's seventy-fifth birthday, Marion invited more than four hundred friends to a costume ball with an American-history theme. The Thalbergs telephoned their acceptance to Marion and said they would arrive in the company of Adrian and his wife, Janet Gaynor; the newly arrived Viennese actress Hedy Lamarr; Mr. and Mrs. Charles Boyer; and the Rathbones. Then Norma telephoned the members of her party to tell them she had arranged with Adrian to have her group select and be fitted in his yet unseen *Marie Antoinette* costumes. "Norma's reasoning, that since Lafayette had contributed so much to the cause of the American revolution made wearing Louis XVI dress appropriate, seemed logical to all of us at the time," Ouida Rathbone would later recall; "but after the ball we were marched off to the tumbrels!"

The day of the gala, Norma sent studio hairdressers and costume dressers to her friends' houses to adjust the women's wigs and help them get into the immense skirts. To accommodate Ouida's gown and tall court wig, the seat of the Rathbones' Rolls was removed, and she sat on blankets. Basil rode up front with the chauffeur as they drove to the Thalbergs', where the party ate a light supper, standing up in their unwieldy apparel. "We could hardly fit into Norma's dining room wearing those huge dresses," Ouida remembered, "and they weighed a ton!" Then, their limousines forming a caravan, the group drove off to Beach House.

Arriving at the height of the festivities, radiant in her organdy gown, decorated and festooned with exquisite silk flowers, her head crowned with a towering white wig enhanced with flowers and jewels, Norma swept across the lighted terrace on her husband's arm. With a gorgeous entourage following them, the Thalbergs created a sensation sufficient to stop the proceedings dead. In the ensuing embarrassed silence, Hearst, who with Marion (dressed as a Pilgrim maid), was receiving guests, stared, turned pale with rage, and strode into the house. Ouida, who had worn the black velvet gown trimmed with gold lace and jeweled embroidery designed for Gladys George as Mme Du Barry, has recalled that "it was ghastly! Hearst spoke to none of us and ordered we be seated at a table in the farthermost corner for supper. Everyone ignored us. Marion glanced over at me sympathetically but indicated she didn't dare to speak. Then, Hedda Hopper pounced on me! She was dressed up as Pocahontas and was carrying a little hatchet which she shook at me and whispered: 'It's the end of all of you!' Poor little Hedy Lamarr couldn't stop crying, and by the time we left I was close to weeping, too."

It took several years and the intercession of numerous friends before Hearst forgave the Rathbones for being innocent accomplices to the Thalbergs' deliberate slap, but he never forgave Norma or Irving. Of course, there were many in Hollywood who were secretly delighted to see the often arrogant Hearst get a comeuppance. After Heast's death, even his "little lady" Marion sometimes retold the story with obvious delight to close friends.

Irving Thalberg died less than a year after the costume ball and before filming began on his grandiose project. With Norma Shearer playing the role he had provided her, the film was not a box-office success, but Cedric Gibbons' art direction and Adrian's costumes gave it lasting historical significance, and it was perhaps the most sumptuous spectacle to come out of Hollywood in the 1930s. Using the dramatic contrasts of black and white for which he was noted, an imaginative interpretation of historical fact, daring proportions, and lavish decorative details, Adrian created movie costumes of heroic grandeur.

Although his costumes for MGM's spectaculars and highbrow comedies delighted audiences, Adrian's finest work was done in the thirties for Greta Garbo, the mysterious beauty who remains the great enigma of the motion picture industry. The combination of Adrian and Garbo was perfect; Adrian re-created for her some of the most famous women of history and fiction, including Queen Christina of Sweden, Mata Hari, and Marguerite in *Camille*. In a 1935 interview, Adrian said of Garbo: "She is a sensitive and very beautiful woman, in a rather spiritual way. I think her eyes are extraordinary and . . . she has a beautiful body, slender and athletic. She rarely ever comes into fittings with her hair combed, never wears makeup except for a dark line at the edge of each eyelid."

For her one appearance at a costume party in Hollywood (she disliked wearing costumes except when she acted), Adrian dressed Garbo as Hamlet, possibly taking his inspiration from the name given the actress by Gertrude Stein: "Mademoiselle Hamlet." Wearing black tights with boots under a black velvet doublet adorned with a gold chain and a pendant of real diamonds and rubies Adrian had rented for the occasion, Garbo never looked more extraordinary. Minutes after her arrival, a photographer snapped her picture, disobeying the

The thirties was the period of white and white in black-and-white movies. Some believe it to have been devised by MGM's talented art director Cedric Gibbons to emphasize the platinum shimmer of star Jean Harlow. Adrian followed this chic trend when in the 1933 production Dinner at Eight *he dressed Harlow almost entirely in white. Here she wears a halter-necked sheath of bias-cut white satin, adorned with immense cuffs trimmed with marabou and rhinestones. A totally outré appearance, Harlow's glittering Christmas-tree image enchanted audiences and helped guide them through the gray Depression years.*

host's strict instructions to the contrary. With head bowed and without uttering a sound, Garbo left.

She departed from films almost as quietly in 1941, after completing her thirty-second picture, *Two-Faced Woman*. Unhappy with the project from the first, Garbo had stoically accepted the direction of George Cukor for a film plagued with problems, one of which was a ridiculous, poorly written script. Adrian again designed Garbo's clothes. He provided her with twenty-eight beautiful ensembles, all of which Cukor refused to accept, insisting that the designs be simplified to have an "off the rack" look. Mayer had decided (with Cukor's support) that Garbo's image had to become more "ordinary," and a deliberate effort was made to deglamorize her and present her as a comedienne with a blander, down-to-earth personality. The designer grudgingly complied and Garbo eventually emerged on the screen with her hair frizzed, wearing woolen sweaters and uninteresting department-store apparel. When the picture was completed, Garbo quietly, but firmly, closed and locked the door on the public and has shielded herself from publicity ever since. *Two-Faced Woman* was a total disaster. Critics decried the new supermarket-housewife look MGM had imposed on Garbo, and cries of "Absurd" . . . "Empty" . . . "Embarrassing," greeted its release. Adrian, still only in his thirties, deserted MGM and the movies and turned to the business of opening his own custom apparel salon.

How much Garbo's decision to retire from movies affected Adrian's own departure from the studio may only be surmised, but in all probability a major factor was slashed budgets. For most of his career, Adrian's salary was a thousand dollars per week, considered a very large amount for the time. Rumors that he might be asked to accept a smaller sum could not have pleased him, and with the new predominance of color films (which Adrian did not enjoy doing), and a new gaudiness of costuming demanded by directors, he must have turned away from movie production with as much distaste as discouragement. He had, however, a kind of revenge when the economy-minded Mayer was forced to hire six designers to replace his one glowing talent.

Irene would become Adrian's successor as executive designer at MGM. One of the most talented designers to ever work in motion pictures, she had been previously well established as a superb dressmaker through her salon-boutique in Bullock's prestigious store in Los Angeles. Evening gowns were her specialty, and her taste for employing fabrics in ingenious ways gave her clothes a sophisticated and timeless quality. Everything she created had a cling or a flow, accentuating the simple, draped lines of her garments, and the stars she dressed were moving sculptures. Among her most successful and noted costumes for various studios were her designs for Constance Bennett in *Topper* (1937), Claudette Colbert in *The Palm Beach Story* (1942), Carole Lombard in *Mr. and Mrs. Smith* (1941), and Loretta Young in *He Stayed for Breakfast* (1940). She remained at MGM until her contract ended in 1949.

While MGM had been basking in the glittering talents of Adrian, Paramount's costume design department had risen to its own pinnacle of splendor. Paramount's first important contract designer had been Howard Greer. Trained in Lucile's elegant custom salons in Chicago, New York, and Paris, Greer was brought from New York to the Far West to lend haute-couture chic to the movies. His costumes for Pola Negri, Nancy Carroll, Bebe Daniels, and Evelyn Brent, who numbered among Paramount's top stars, were original and extravagant in conception and execution. Greer was the first Hollywood designer to establish a workroom in the tradition of a French dressmaking house, and he insisted on perfection in the making of his designs. But in 1927, after four years made legendary by his temperamental antics (encouraged by an addiction to alcohol), Greer refused to renew his contract with Paramount and opened his own salon. He continued to design on a free-lance basis until 1953, but his real allegiance had always been to the kind of couture he had worked on with Lucile. For many years he successfully presented three collections a year to a wealthy Hollywood clientele.

Garbo's role as the legendary love-struck monarch in Queen Christina (MGM, 1933) was made especially memorable by the designs that Adrian created for her. For much of the picture she is dressed in masculine trousers and boots, or in relatively plain gowns. Even her regal coronation dress is somewhat underplayed, with its broad bands of jeweled fabric and lack of frills. Garbo very obviously stands out from the women around her.

In Mata Hari (MGM, 1932), as the infamous but irresistible spy of World War I, Greta Garbo appeared in some of the most extravagant costumes Adrian ever concocted.

Garbo's Byzantine-looking bugle-beaded skull cap, designed by Adrian, was hung with glittering disks.

Garbo as Camille *in the film no studio has since dared remake—romantic, poignant, exquisitely costumed by Adrian (MGM, 1936).*

Columbia's 1941 production of Bedtime Story *starred Loretta Young in this costume by Irene.*

Carole Lombard in a gown designed by Irene for RKO's Mr. and Mrs. Smith *(1941).*

Howard Greer, who had been Paramount's chief designer from 1923 to 1927, returned there seven years later to design most of the costumes for Sylvia Sidney in Thirty Day Princess. Here, sketch in hand, he beams happily at the star, who is modeling one of his gowns.

Norma Talmadge modeling a Greer design.

For Ginger Rogers in RKO's 1939 Fifth Avenue Girl, *Howard Greer designed a classically cut princess-style evening gown of shimmering lamé. The simplicity of his conception for Miss Rogers was a welcome change from the fountains of feathers and flounces, and acres of pleated chiffon she usually appeared in. Indeed, Greer succeeded in giving her a true "Fifth Avenue" kind of elegance.*

A 1941 Universal publicity portrait of Irene Dunne for her appearance in Unfinished Business demonstrates Howard Greer's ability to design smart elegant clothes. Using one of his favorite devices, a soft sleeve tapering to the wrist (in this case, with moderately rounded padded shoulders), he underlined the level-headed yet benevolent qualities that Miss Dunne projected from the screen to her countless fans. The boldly printed crêpe he has used works well because of the highly controlled manner in which it is cut.

Paramount replaced Greer with Travis Banton, an assistant to Mme Francis of New York, whose original designs were much in demand by actresses of the Broadway theater. Walter Wanger had discovered Banton and brought him to the studio on a one-picture deal to costume The Dressmaker from Paris (1925). Banton's designs were so successful that Zukor signed him as chief designer and he was given Greer's former sketch artist, Edith Head, as his assistant.

Travis Banton's understated and deceptively simple designs elevated motion picture costumes to the status of high fashion. His innate understanding of the bias cut originated earlier by the French couturière Madeleine Vionnet and his sense of exquisite balance in a garment perfectly captured the new sophistication that arrived with the thirties. A Banton gown, with a softness and sultriness that followed a woman's body, was Hollywood design at its most sublime.

In the mid-thirties Paramount's Carole Lombard, Lilyan Tashman, Gail Patrick, Miriam Hopkins, Kay Francis, and Claudette Colbert were the most distinctively dressed women in the movies. And of course there was the irrepressible Mae West, for whom Banton produced a series of lush pastiche gowns of the Gay Nineties that matched the star's wit and worldly wisdom. When Banton's very full schedule prevented him from personally dressing Paramount's curvaceous Miss West, the versatile Edith Head performed this assignment with admirable results and endeared herself to the star, who thereafter requested that "little Eadie" costume her.

Had Banton designed only for Marlene Dietrich, he would have been assured fame as a great movie magician. The German director Josef Von Sternberg brought Dietrich to Paramount in 1930 after his German-made film *The Blue Angel* revealed the plump Berlin cabaret singer's potential as an important glamour-property. In truth, the "orchid of Paramount" was a personal creation of Von Sternberg's, who was helped immensely in his miraculous transformation of the hefty Fräulein by Banton's ability to sense and exploit her unique qualities. Working with Von Sternberg, Banton made her his special triumph, one that astonished producers, cameramen, and the public alike. The costumes he created for her in *Morocco* (1930), *Shanghai Express* (1932), *Blonde Venus* (1932), *The Devil Is a Woman* (1935), *Desire* (1936), and *Angel* (1937) were marvels of extravagant mystery. Swathed in chiffon or mountains of fur, or suited impeccably in white tie and tails, or with her head and shoulders encircled by lustrous black coq feathers, Dietrich was overwhelmingly beautiful.

As Catherine of Russia in Sternberg's 1934 *The Scarlet Empress* (a rare instance in which Dietrich and Banton were joined for a period film), Dietrich wore a series of gorgeous albeit not historically accurate ensembles. Two of them are especially memorable: a pale pink satin dress with wide panniers banded with clouds of ostrich feathers, and a white hussar's uniform (with tights and short white gold-tasseled boots) in which she made an unforgettable gallop on the back of a white horse up the stairs of the strange palace designed by Paramount's famed art director, Hans Dreier. Though more restrained in the use of glitter and gold, Banton's re-creations of the Empress of All the Russias were rivaled by Adrian's for Norma Shearer as Marie Antoinette four years later.

Banton's predilection for extravagant materials was encouraged by Adolph Zukor, the founder and head of Paramount, who spared nothing to see that his stars were dressed in the manner the public had come to expect. Zukor had once been a successful furrier in Chicago and his admiration for fur was expressed in the directives he sent Banton advising him to use a lavish hand in applying it to his costumes. Banton happily responded by giving his creations wide cuffs, collars, and borders of fur, and fur muffs, hats, and scarves as accessories whenever possible. The designer used yards of mink, sable, ermine, and chinchilla to romanticize Dietrich, and draped the plump shoulders of Mae West with triple-skin scarves of white fox. One beige velvet evening wrap that Dietrich wore for a series of publicity photographs featured a high collar, cuffs, and a hem bordered with red fox. Twenty-three skins were required.

Claudette Colbert as she appeared in The Gilded Lily *(Paramount, 1935), in a costume by Travis Banton.*

The original caption for this 1926 publicity photograph read: "Travis Banton, who creates the ultra-chic costumes for all Paramount's stars, including Ruth Taylor in the picture, says that coats and evening wraps will shrink to a position just below the hip-line, and that skirts will terminate somewhere in the area of the ankle. The black chiffon gown and silver jacket trimmed with sable have received Banton's enthusiastic okay." It was Banton who costumed Miss Taylor for Anita Loos' heroine in Gentlemen Prefer Blondes. *Shortly after the film's release, Miss Taylor proved the truth of its title by retiring from the screen to marry (naturally) a millionaire!*

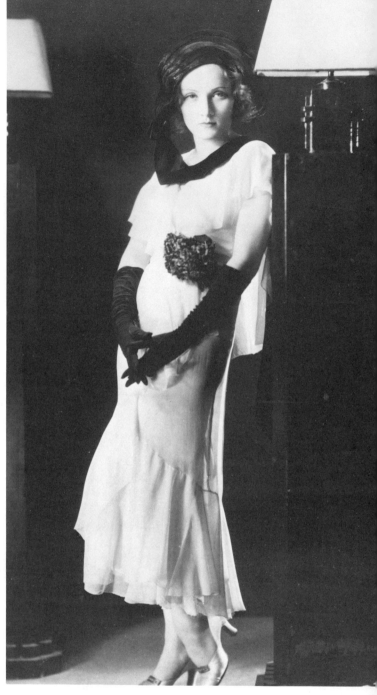

Travis Banton designed this dress for Dietrich for the film Morocco *(Paramount, 1930).*

One of Banton's creations worn by Carole Lombard in Paramount's Sinners in the Sun *(1932).*

Paramount's 1932 tale of love and danger aboard the Shanghai Express had the inscrutable Dietrich in one of her most exotic roles—an international delight known around the Near, Middle, and Far East as Shanghai Lily. For stalking the corridors of the intrigue-laden wagon-lits, Travis Banton disguised her as a black swan, hidden in a jungle of coq feathers, veiled, and hung with a rope of glittering crystal beads. Dietrich's handbag and gloves in this scene were specially made for her by Hermès at the request of Banton, loose on one of his frequent shopping sprees in Paris.

Marlene Dietrich often chose to wear masculine clothes off screen as well as on. For a Hollywood function in the mid-1930s, Miss Dietrich wore this Banton-designed suit with its broad shoulders, smart lapels, and man's shirt and tie, creating something of a sensation. Other actresses tried to emulate her style, but only the exceptional Marlene could carry off such a feat and maintain her inimitable femininity.

Marlene Dietrich, here gowned superbly by Travis Banton for Paramount's 1935 Desire. *Swathed, draped, enveloped in chiffon that flowed about her like the rippling waters about a fountain goddess, Dietrich captured the imagination and heart of audiences with an allure that has never been equaled.*

Banton's sketch for the gown from Desire *is itself an expression of the serene, sensuous classicism that dominated fashion illustration during the 1930s.*

Dietrich as the screen's most beautiful Catherine the Great—in The Scarlet Empress, Paramount's 1934 film for which Travis Banton designed a series of wonderful make-believe eighteenth-century confections. Banton's love of the extravagant had full play, and although his designs for Dietrich's gowns left everything to be desired historically, as pure examples of Hollywood costuming at its most lush and lovely they were superb interpretations. (Note Marlene's magnificent Cartier bracelet of diamonds and emeralds, rented for the film, as were her rings and hair clip.)

One of Orry-Kelly's favorite touches was hand-painted fabric, a device he used in this dress worn by Marion Davies in Page Miss Glory *(Warner Brothers, 1935). Advised by Jack Warner to spare no expense on her costumes, the designer in this instance seems to have gotten carried away. While the side-paneled train adds a touch of grandeur, it is difficult to find an explanation for the bouquets of flowers sprouting egret feathers surrounding her tightly coiffed head and showgirl smile. As Miss Davies is placed on a dais with baskets of more flowers, one can only applaud Kelly's boldness and assume he held his tongue in his cheek for this project.*

Ranking close to Adrian and Banton was designer Orry-Kelly, who undertook direction of the Warner Brothers costume design department in 1932. After a brief career designing clothes for Broadway actresses, Kelly came to California and quickly established himself at Warners as a talented, versatile designer suited to dressing the feminine stars Jack Warner presented. His special favorites were Bette Davis, Olivia de Havilland, Kay Francis, Mary Astor, Ingrid Bergman, and Rosalind Russell.

But it was for Bette Davis that he did his most successful work. She was not easy to costume. Aware of the fact that she had a less than perfect figure, Miss Davis cooperated with Kelly when he required her to wear specially designed corsets or brassieres to mold her silhouette into the proper shape for a period role. However, when it came to wearing contemporary clothes for a film with a modern setting, Miss Davis was adamant about being unencumbered by elaborate undergarments, and her full bosom and plumpish figure presented problems. With the skill of an engineer, Kelly restructured her figure with cleverly cut, well-made garments that successfully created the desired image. Miss Davis's penchant for changing her appearance with each new role presented a tremendous challenge to those involved with preparing her for the camera.

For period films, however, Davis and Kelly worked together with superb rapport. Each strove for accuracy, and discomfort was forgotten for the star's appearance in such unforgettable films as *Jezebel* (1938), *The Old Maid* (1939), *The Private Lives of Elizabeth and Essex* (1939), and *The Little Foxes* (Samuel

Here Bette Davis appears as a Southern belle in Jezebel *(Warner Brothers, 1938), wearing Orry-Kelly's soft white gown of tulle and lace (to suggest youth and innocence).*

Davis was cast as the ruthless but beautiful Regina Giddens in The Little Foxes *(Samuel Goldwyn, 1941). Her mature-looking gown of heavy crocheted lace and her upswept hair clearly reflect her character's hard personality in the film.*

One of the greatest strengths in many of the roles played by Bette Davis was Orry-Kelly's costuming. As Elizabeth I of England in The Private Lives of Elizabeth and Essex *(Warner Brothers, 1939), she wore this outfit with large collars and cuffs that seemed to convey her power. Miss Davis, who never shied from doing whatever was necessary for the sake of authenticity, allowed the hair above her forehead to be shaved so she might better resemble her historical counterpart.*

Bette Davis in a costume by Orry-Kelly for Mr. Skeffington *(Warner Brothers, 1944).*

Goldwin, 1941). In period design, Kelly followed fact more closely than did his peers Adrian and Banton (who both immensely respected his work) and stressed perfectly-executed dressmaker's trimming and fine handwork. Embroidery and appliqué were kept on a smaller scale than that used by Adrian, and the historical *shape* of the garments was strictly adhered to. When production chief Hal Wallis insisted that Miss Davis wear smaller farthingales in *The Private Lives of Elizabeth and Essex* than the true queen had worn, Davis winked at Kelly and wore a smaller hoop for the costume test photographs, which Wallis approved. When she stepped before the camera, however, the star wore hoops of the proper size.

In a sense, Orry-Kelly bridged the gap between realism and the exaggerated world of the movies with greater success than his theatrically oriented rivals did. Boisterous, temperamental, addicted to alcohol, often almost impossible to work with, overshadowed by Adrian and Banton, Orry-Kelly must nonetheless be acknowledged as one of Hollywood's most important and astute costume designers. After he had left Warner Brothers in 1944 to open a private business, faithful Bette Davis wrote that "it was like losing my right arm."

Among Hollywood designers who worked for a major studio during the thirties, Edith Head is unique. Her career, more than any other designer's, presents a success story that would make an excellent scenario. Having begun at Paramount in 1923 as a sketch artist for Howard Greer, the diminutive Edith became Travis Banton's assistant when Greer left the studio. A great admirerer of Banton, she has said: "Travis was a marvelous designer. Any talent I might have would have lain undiscovered if he hadn't lighted the way for me. In my opinion, he was the greatest." Gradually, Banton had assigned certain stars he did not have the time to design for (or did not like personally) to his young assistant, and when he retired from Paramount in 1938, Miss Head was named chief designer, a title she would hold there for twenty-nine years.

Miss Head's successes are far too numerous to enumerate; let it suffice to say that she has, perhaps more than any other designer for the movies, influenced fashion trends for more than five decades. In 1936 she wrapped Paramount's pseudo–South Seas beauty Dorothy Lamour in a boldly patterned sarong. Modestly pagan, Head's wraparound design was immediately adapted by bathing-suit manufacturers and Head's name became a household word. The following season, women of all shapes and sizes could be seen on beaches from Coney Island to Cannes reclining on the sands in Miss Lamour's exotic attire. "Fashion Goes Native!" *Silver Screen* magazine declared. "Have you the secret wish to become a beautiful island enchantress? Well, lovely Dorothy Lamour's slinky native sarongs will soon be available to every plain Jane! This delectable creation (that accents one's most feminine qualities) has swooped fashion to new romantic heights."

In 1974, Miss Lamour would tell a writer: "I played dozens of roles and wore lots of beautiful clothes, but when people thought of Lamour, she was always wearing one of Edith's 'jungle kimonos.' . . . They became a trademark. I

75

could never seem to get out of them. Even today, when people meet me for the first time, I think they expect me to be wearing one."

Head also started a fashion rage when she gave Audrey Hepburn a simple self-tied boat-neck linen afternoon dress in Paramount's 1954 *Sabrina* (for which Head won that year's Academy Award for costume design) that was widely copied by New York dress manufacturers. Her simple *jeune fille* designs for Elizabeth Taylor in several films also greatly influenced fashion trends in America for several generations of young women.

On occasion, mainly for promotional value, a major studio would hire a renowned French designer for a special star or fashion-oriented production. Such a practice, however, was never really successful as, for the most part, couture apparel did not photograph as dramatically as designs created in Hollywood. Paramount's 1937 *Artists and Models Abroad,* with Jack Benny, Joan Bennett, and Gail Patrick, was such a fashion-show extravaganza. In it Travis Banton's gowns were supplemented by a parade of gowns created in Paris by Pacquin, Worth, Jean Patou, Schiaparelli, Maggy Rouff, Lanvin, and Alix. Edith Head was also a contributor to the great number of constumes required for this haute couture comedy-spectacle. Unfortunately, many of the dresses from France had to be revamped somewhat to give them the kind of glamorous impact movie audiences had come to expect on the screen.

The elegantly casual look of the esteemed Gabrielle Chanel was also brought to Hollywood movies when, at the urging of Gloria Swanson, she was signed to costume three films in the thirties, including one of Swanson's first talkies, *Tonight or Never* (1931). The aloof Mme Chanel was welcomed to Hollywood with the same kind of roses-and-champagne fanfare that had greeted Erté in an earlier year. Chanel's wardrobe for the chic Miss Swanson was elaborate and very expensive. It included an afternoon ensemble of black satin lavished with ermine and a satin evening gown with a wide collar and immense cuffs of sable. Another evening gown, made of black velvet with diamond and emerald brooches, was worn under a full-length evening coat cuffed and bordered with a fortune in chinchilla.

Despite such luxurious conceptions, Chanel's designs did not bridge the distance between her Rue Cambon salon and the movies. Their failure as film costumes pointed up the differences between the worlds of high fashion and of fantasy-fashion created expressly for motion pictures. Chanel had stated that she believed Hollywood overdressed its stars; she came to California determined to put her couture on the screen exactly as it was created for her clients in Paris. Instead, her understated garments seemed drab and unexciting when photographed and magnified on a screen. Up to the time of her death in 1971, however, Chanel's clothes would occasionally appear in European films. (Delphine Seyrig was dressed by Chanel for her 1961 film, *Last Year at Marienbad,* and in 1962, the German actress Romy Schneider wore Chanel clothes to superb effect in *Boccaccio '70.*)

Schiaparelli also became involved with the movie industry when Paramount

The last stage in the creation of a costume: Edith Head checks the final effect of Joan Bennett's dinner suit against her original sketch.

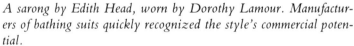

A sarong by Edith Head, worn by Dorothy Lamour. Manufacturers of bathing suits quickly recognized the style's commercial potential.

commissioned her to dress their box-office queen, Mae West, in the 1937 film *Every Day's a Holiday*. The eccentric Italian-born designer refused to sail the Atlantic and cross America by train to supervise the making of her designs, however, and Miss West was determined to remain in her ninth-floor penthouse at the Ravenswold (where she still lives), an apartment building six blocks from the Paramount lot. To compromise, Paramount sent a copy of their star's dress form to Paris. But the copy had been inadequately padded, it was later discovered, and Schiaparelli's lavish creations arrived at the wardrobe department inches too small to accommodate West's Rubensian curves. Working feverishly and at great cost, the studio's wardrobe staff remade the entire set of costumes to meet the film's schedule. The clever Schiaparelli profited handsomely from the deal by adapting the hourglass shape of West's dress dummy to a perfume

This elegant gown was designed by Maggy Rouff for the fashion show sequence in Paramount's Artists and Models Abroad *(1937).*

Gabrielle Chanel first brought her elegant fashions to Hollywood in the thirties. She costumed Gloria Swanson in the 1931 film Tonight or Never.

bottle that she labeled Shocking, to describe her impression of the silhouette. The success of the perfume and the shocking pink color of a ribbon on the bottle that was introduced into Schiaparelli's collection the following year became part of fashion history.

The greatest phenomenon of the entertainment industry in the thirties was the introduction of the movie musical extravaganza. Pure fantasy and visually beyond the limits of anything previously offered audiences, the Hollywood film musical opened the floodgates of imagination to release a wave of gorgeous make-believe. It answered America's growing need for a form of escape from the problems that beset the nation while it attempted to struggle out of the worst depression

For Every Day's a Holiday, *a 1937 vehicle for Paramount's Mae West, the Italian-born couturière Elsa Schiaparelli agreed to have a go at Hollywood. Long before the days of jet travel, Mme Schiaparelli refused to desert her salon on the Place Vendôme for the workrooms at Paramount. Instead, an exact replica of Miss West was shipped off to France and everyone sat back and waited with wondering expectation. When the completed gowns at last arrived, to the horror of everyone concerned they proved to be much too small for the curvaceous Mae to manage. Working furiously, the Paramount wardrobe staff remade Schiaparelli's entire collection in time for filming. Here is Mae, wearing one of the designer's rather lingerielike creations of chiffon and Chantilly lace with a frothing of ostrich fronds. Pure Hollywood. But the headdress—pure Folies Bergère! Her adoring gentleman friend is the suave Edmund Lowe.*

in modern times. The movie musical caused a westward migration of thousands of Broadway's out-of-work vaudeville and nightclub performers.

One of the most memorable of the new full-blown sound musicals was Warner Brothers' 1933 production *Forty-Second Street,* starring Ruby Keeler and Dick Powell. The standard tale of a chorus girl who rises to stardom when she is asked to replace a star who has broken her ankle on the opening night of a Broadway musical, *Forty-Second Street* was an astounding success. The following year, one of the chorus girls in the film, Ginger Rogers, became Fred Astaire's dancing partner in RKO's *Flying Down to Rio,* thus beginning the movies' most famous dance team.

Astaire and Rogers seemed to dance for each other alone, romantically, in an elegant, enchanted world. Their feet made magic on moonlit terraces, empty ballrooms with black-mirror floors, and the decks of yachts at midnight. "They looked like the dream couple on top of a wedding cake who had stepped down to dance for us. You knew at once they were headed for a happy ending," Anita Loos has said. Fred's impeccable white tie and tails and Ginger's flowing, diaphanous gowns were an inspiration to an entire generation that danced cheek-to-cheek to the music of the Big Bands. The image was conveyed perfectly in the words of a popular song of the day: "Moonlight becomes you, it goes with your hair, you certainly know the right thing to wear."

At the same time, audiences were gasping at each new and more astounding musical concocted by Hollywood. Expanded far beyond the production excesses of Barnum or Ziegfeld, gargantuan dream orgies unfolded on the screens across America. Dream girls were the major element; they dallied beneath cascading waterfalls like cellophane-draped sirens, drifted down stairways or ascended them to the stars, waltzed in wide tiered skirts of organdy playing neon-lighted violins, tap danced on the keys of mountainous grand pianos. Wearing satin shorts and goggled helmets, the lithesome ladies fearlessly danced on the wings of airplanes high above the bay of Rio, or lived it up at masquerade balls held in the lounge of a Zeppelin in the mid-Atlantic.

Busby Berkeley, brought from Broadway to choreograph MGM musicals in 1932, was the Merlin of the movie musical. Berkeley transferred to Warner Brothers in the same year he arrived and there continued to exploit every known possibility of movie production. Décor and costumes reached new heights of splendor, photographed by cameras that could swing and move with the agility of a bird.

Of all the innovations in the film-making industry during the thirties, none was so important as the advent of Technicolor. Accustomed to working in the colorless world of black-and-white film, Hollywood designers thought, sketched their ideas, and saw the results of their creations in a netural-colored atmosphere. When color was used, it was applied to costume sketches to dramatize a designer's idea and make it easier to receive a director's or star's approval. Thus it often happened that costumes made for black-and-white films were executed in bizarre, even hideous, color combinations: lavender and orange, olive green and mustard, magenta and lemon yellow. It was the way a color *photographed* that mattered; what tone of gray it produced on film was the sole determinant of its use.

Adrian was a master of this limited palette. His black-and-white films suggest color in miraculous ways; audiences always sensed when Crawford was wearing red, Shearer a delicate pastel, or Garbo a deep, moody color. He also delighted in strong contrasts between light and dark that added drama to a figure, and it is significant that he stated that he did not enjoy working for color film, that it distracted and annoyed him to deal with the new techniques the process required.

The often-told but exemplary story of the famous red dress designed by Orry-Kelly and worn by Bette Davis in Warner Brothers' 1938 *Jezebel* serves to illustrate how a movie designer could conjure up the illusion of a particular color in a black-and-white medium. The gown was crucial to the development of the film's plot. Davis, as a petulant Southern belle, agrees to attend a fashionable cotillion ball—for which the women guests had been requested to wear a white gown. Instead, the character chooses to appear in bright red, much to the consternation of a proper antebellum society.

Kelly made a costume from the brightest red satin he could find, but in subsequent costume tests it appeared listless and dull. After considerable experimentation, the perfect "color" was achieved with a rust-brown fabric; the resulting gown was so successful it became Kelly's most famous creation. Generally, Kelly used fabrics that had a base color of a warm tone (brown, mustard, muted purple, or dull orange) to achieve the particularly rich grays his designs photographed on film. He humorously referred to his color range as consisting of "varying shades of muck."

The first successful color film was *Becky Sharp* (1935). An adaptation of Thackeray's novel *Vanity Fair,* it was the first feature-length picture to be made entirely in the newly developed three-color Technicolor process. Directed by Rouben Mamoulian and starring Miriam Hopkins in the title role, the film had sets and costumes designed by the genius of the New York stage, Robert Edmond Jones. The film was a stunning demonstration of the possibilities of color photography and created a mild sensation that at once jeopardized the future of black-and-white movies. (Among the group of extras who appeared in a ball sequence in the film was a young woman who later became the wife of Richard M. Nixon.)

By 1939, when Adrian costumed MGM's *The Wizard of Oz,* Technicolor had reached a high degree of development, though it still presented drawbacks for a designer. Hues and tints in early color films could be erratic—either too harsh and intense, or as pale as a faint wash. In particular, pale blues almost completely disappeared, whereas bright blue leaped from the screen with a blinding brilliance. Yellow might become greenish or cadmium orange in hue, depending on the amount of light it received when photographed. A white costume surrounded by colored ones photographed as a blur of brightness and needed to be softened by a bath of light gray dye, a process known as teccing. Charts showing numerous numbered samples of gray became a standard reference for costume designers working on color films. The designer could select from fifty such tones. He would then confer with the movie's photographer, and the costume would be tagged for dyeing (Tec. 14, for instance, indicated it was to receive a bath of the gray shade numbered 14). It was a long and often frustrating process, one which designers generally delegated to their assistants.

Trained color experts were hired by the studios to assist designers in coping with this new problem. Most designers who had begun their film careers designing in black-and-white never satisfactorily adjusted to the new innovation, and both Adrian and Banton expressed their preference for working in the achromatic medium.

A typically surreal production number from one of the thirties' musical extravaganzas.

Though every major studio in Hollywood during the thirties had a resident chief designer, most also availed themselves of the services offered by a large number of free-lancers like Omar Kiam, Earl Luick, Herschel, Robert Kalloch, and Howard Shoup.

Twentieth Century-Fox in particular used free-lance designers for "fill-in," generally on one-picture contracts, but the studio's main costume responsibilities were delegated to Royer (Lewis Royer Hastings) from 1933 to 1939 and the versatile and talented Gwen Wakeling (1935–42). Miss Wakeling, who had been discovered by Cecil B. De Mille and worked for him both at Pathé and Paramount during the twenties, also worked on a free-lance basis for Columbia, United Artists, Republic, Warner Brothers, and RKO, between 1942 and 1965.

Bernard Newman designed Ginger Rogers' famous ice-blue ostrich-feather dance gown for Top Hat, a 1935 RKO production. Her leading man and dance partner, the ultrasophisticated Fred Astaire, is said to have objected strongly to the sometimes overdressed Ginger's outfits, complaining there was too much feathery froth and flurry for him to endure during their dance routines. Newman's gown remained, however, and for all purposes worked wonderfully well. In time Miss Rogers would declare the gown to be one of her favorite film costumes. Mr. Astaire has genteelly refused to discuss the matter.

Seen wearing a platinum-blond wig, Ruby Keeler strokes a neon-edged white violin, surrounded by an ensemble of earnest musicians gowned in swirling triple-tiered skirts. One of the dreamland sequences in Warner Brothers' Gold Diggers of 1933, such fantasies of movie kitsch were irresistible to audiences everywhere and elevated the American musical film to a supreme form of popular entertainment.

Bette Davis wearing Orry-Kelly's strapless red satin ball gown in Warner Brothers' 1938 Jezebel, *the tale of a Southern beauty much like Scarlett O'Hara, who was still to come to the screen. For this black-and-white film, Kelly experimented for days seeking a color red that would suggest scarlet in a gray tone. After numerous tests, a medium reddish-brown color proved to be the most successful. This costume was vitally important to the story line of the movie. When Bette Davis's character defied tradition and wore the gown to an all-white cotillion, she lost her fiancé Henry Fonda, who was so shocked by her daring he left town the following morning. In the end he did return, married to another woman and racked with yellow fever. The reformed Jezebel begs to accompany the dying Fonda to a quarantined island, and, cradling him in her arms, rides off to glory—a heroine in the great movie tradition. And all because she* would *wear that dress!*

Left: The Great Ziegfeld, *MGM's 1936 extravaganza loosely based on the life and loves of the prince of Broadway producers, combined the talents of Busby Berkeley, Cedric Gibbons, and Adrian. The trio concocted such spectacles as this: masses of black bugle-beaded showgirls impersonating cats, with a chorus of tailcoated and top-hatted men singing lustily to the accompaniment of countless mighty Wurlitzers, all frosted with white-gowned showgirls daintily arranged on immense sections of revolving Doric columns. It was a sight to make Louis B. Mayer beam with contentment, for it fulfilled his vision of the kind of class he wanted to bring to Americans everywhere.*

The designer Royer dressed Shirley Temple for Baby Take a Bow *(Twentieth Century-Fox, 1934).*

Billie Burke and Judy Garland in The Wizard of Oz, *costumed by Adrian.*

This talented design team was joined by Herschel in 1936, and for six years, the three of them costumed the numerous low-budget B pictures that were Fox's bread-and-butter products. Most of Herschel's time was spent costuming films built around the two Oriental crime sleuths Mr. Moto and Charlie Chan, while Royer and Wakeling worked to see that the studio's leading star, Loretta

Marlene Dietrich, here in a design by Vera West for the 1942 Universal film The Spoilers.

In Universal Pictures' 1941 Nice Girl? *Deanna Durbin personified for millions of teen-age fans what every young lady longed to be—happy, healthy, sweet as homemade ice cream, and able to sing a romantic ballad or face a one hundred piece symphony orchestra conducted by Leopold Stokowski. This spangled white organdy dress designed by Vera West, suitably ruffled and modestly cut, set the fashion for young girls at prom dances and country-club parties across America. Immensely popular abroad as well as in America, a similar photograph of Miss Durbin, clipped from a movie magazine of the time, may still be seen pasted above Anne Frank's tiny bed in the secret quarters in which she and her family were hidden in Nazi-occupied Amsterdam, a poignant reminder of the temporary escape a movie star might bring to a girl engulfed by horrendous circumstances.*

Young, maintained the fresh, clean-cut image her public adored. Herschel would later distinguish himself at MGM, where he was nominated for Academy Awards for *Quo Vadis* (1951) and *Dream Wife* (shared with Helen Rose, 1953). Royer and Wakeling also were responsible for costuming the popular Alice Faye for her nineteenth-century musical romance *In Old Chicago* (1938) and *Rose of Washington Square* (1939), a musical with overtones of Fanny Brice. It was Royer who created Shirley Temple's ruffled dresses in *Baby Take a Bow* (1934); the "cutie-pie" frocks worn by the child star were then mass produced and marketed by a manufacturer who shared the profits with Shirley's parents, much to the designer's dismay.

By 1939, Fox's financial situation, which had suffered from the blow of the depression, had greatly improved, and more and more work was demanded from its designers. Unable to continue under the growing strain, Royer and Wakeling allowed their contracts to expire and left to open a custom salon together, though Wakeling returned to Fox off and on over the years to work on a free-lance basis. At their departure, Travis Banton, Paramount's former king of fashion, was signed as Fox's head designer. He remained until 1941, when Charles LeMaire, a former vaudeville actor who had turned to costume design for Broadway, became executive designer and director of wardrobe, a post he held until 1959. Under his tenure, free-lance designers Oleg Cassini, Kay Nelson, Eleanor Behm, René Hubert, Bonnie Cashin, William Travilla, Edward Stevenson, Perkins Bailey, Renie, Elois Jenssen, Mario Vanarelli, Ursula Maes, Miles White, Mary Wills, Yvonne Wood, Helen Rose, Adele Balkan, Leah Rhodes, and Adele Palmer all shared costume design credits with him, surely a record of some sort.

Universal Pictures was the beneficiary of Vera West's considerable talents. As chief designer from 1927 to 1947, the highly versatile Miss West created flattering and attractive designs that lent taste and distinction to the studio's stars. Before coming to Hollywood, West had designed for a Fifth Avenue salon, where she claims she learned how to get along with rich, often spoiled women who demanded special attention. This ability was to be an asset during her years with Universal and made her one of Hollywood's best-liked designers, although she was rarely requested to do the best films. Among West's most memorable costumes were those for Irene Dunne in *Showboat* (1936), for Deanna Durbin in *Mad About Music* (1938), and for Marlene Dietrich in *Destry Rides Again* (1939) and *The Spoilers* (1942).

Walter Plunkett was named chief designer for RKO in 1926; except for several brief absences when he free-lanced, he remained there until 1939. Considered by many to be Hollywood's most astute period designer, Plunkett costumed every conceivable kind of film and established himself as one of the movies' most versatile and talented artisans. It was he who created the costumes for the delicious early Astaire and Rogers dance musicals *Flying Down to Rio* (1933) and *The Gay Divorcee* (1934). He also designed *Morning Glory* (1933) and *Little Women* (1933), which starred the demanding Katharine Hepburn; his working relationship with the actress was to last for many years. Plunkett's most important assignment,

Katharine Hepburn, costumed by Walter Plunkett for RKO's 1936 adaptation of Maxwell Anderson's Broadway success Mary of Scotland. *Considered by many to be Hollywood's best period-costume designer, Plunkett created a simple but effective wardrobe for Hepburn as the doomed queen. Notice the exquisite detailing of embroidery, the perfectly proportioned neck ruff, and the charming heart-shaped cap, framing Hepburn's superbly constructed face to great advantage.*

however, and one which was the envy of most studio designers, was *Gone With the Wind* (1939).

Gone With the Wind was produced in Technicolor at a cost of $4.2 million by the private impresario David O. Selznick. The brilliant William Cameron Menzies was chosen to design the sets, and Max Steiner was asked to compose the film score (which would become a familiar classic of movie music). Selznick's famous search for a Scarlett engendered such publicity that it became a national issue. Every top Hollywood actress had been invited to make a screen test for Margaret Mitchell's fascinating heroine. Her transition from a spoiled but enchanting ingenue to a bitter, dirty-faced war orphan who ruthlessly and single-handedly climbs to a life of opulent but loveless security was a dream-come-true role for a star. Although Selznick's choice of the English stage actress Vivien Leigh caused cries of protest at the time—"America's fans muster for a new revolution," announced a movie magazine—it is difficult to imagine any Hollywood actress of the time who could have brought Scarlett to the screen with more vibrancy.

Selznick was a perfectionist who insisted that the costumes for *Gone With the Wind* be historically accurate, and still capture the sweeping romanticism of Mitchell's epic of the Civil War and the South's Reconstruction years. It was a difficult and risky assignment to undertake, for if Plunkett had proved less than equal the challenge, his career in Hollywood would have been jeopardized. But Selznick's choice proved to be the right one—Plunkett's re-creation of the period remains an almost perfect example of motion picture period costuming.

Scarlett's wardrobe was a masterpiece of sensitive design that underlined her complex character with subtlety and originality. Plunkett's costumes clearly reflected the two different periods of the heroine's life—the petulant Southern belle, and later the postbellum woman who turns her back on her earlier life of picture-book elegance to face despair, poverty, and the bare necessity to survive. Selznick emphasized the change in Scarlett's character and position by breaking the story with an intermission at the moment the heroine rises from the mud of her devastated Tara to swear revenge on a fate that has robbed her of her secure life. The second phase of Scarlett's wardrobe begins with her ripping apart her mother's dining-room portieres and ordering her mammy (unforgettably portrayed by Hattie McDaniel) to cut them up to make a sweeping gown in which she is determined to enchant and ensnare the rich, sardonic gambler, Rhett Butler, who has the means to pay the inflated taxes on Tara and save it from foreclosure. Plunkett had a bolt of green velvet faded to appear like worn curtains and from it he fashioned the dress which he would later admit was "probably the most famous movie costume ever made."

Plunkett would continue to dress Scarlett in velvet as a kind of leitmotif suggesting her dramatic rise to more affluent circumstances: a velvet bolero jacket with a daytime ensemble, emerald-green velvet lavished with gold embroidery for a dressing gown, sapphire-blue velvet trimmed with black fox for an at-home dress, and garnet-colored velvet decorated with paste rubies and ostrich feathers for an evening dress Rhett contemptuously throws at her after her love for Ashley Wilkes has been discovered. Contrasted with the organdy and tulle dresses worn by Scarlett in the film's first section, these sumptuous garments became dramatic devices that are integral to the film's unfolding action. Plunkett's contribution to *Gone With the Wind* was a Hollywood tour de force and established him as dean among his peers.

Plunkett's replacement as chief designer at RKO was Bernard Newman. A successful designer of custom apparel for Bergdorf Goodman in New York, Newman had been brought to the attention of RKO's management by Irene Dunne after he created a number of gowns for her personal wardrobe and designed for her on a free-lance basis for a number of her films in the thirties. In 1934 he was responsible for the large number of gowns needed for the 1935 fashion musical *Roberta,* which starred Irene Dunne. He worked with another New York custom designer, Muriel King, on the 1935 Katharine Hepburn film *Sylvia Scarlett,* King designing for Hepburn, Newman for Natalie Paley. He dressed Dunne again in *Theodora Goes Wild* (1936) and in the same year gave Ginger Rogers the heavy-beaded dance dress she wore in *Follow the Fleet* with Fred Astaire. The dress had long full sleeves that struck Astaire across the face as he and Rogers danced—much to his chagrin—and though he protested in no uncertain terms, the gown remained in the film and he grinned and bore this assault, though he never forgave Ginger. This episode may have been the beginning of the feud Astaire and Rogers were said to have waged off-screen for years to come.

Not an easy person to work with, and unhappy with the ever-increasing responsibilities placed on him (between 1935 and 1936 he worked on nearly twenty films), Newman resigned from RKO in 1936 to return to New York. He went back to RKO on a free-lance basis in 1937 to design for Ginger Rogers in *Vivacious Lady* (1938), and also worked on short-term contracts with Warner Brothers, where he did *Deception* (1946) with Bette Davis and *Dark Passage* (1947) with Lauren Bacall. He then resumed his career as head designer for Bergdorf's custom salon.

Newman's successor at RKO was Edward Stevenson. Born in Idaho in 1906, Stevenson came to Hollywood in 1922, studied fashion illustration, and in 1925 became a sketch artist at MGM. In 1927 he became an assistant designer at Fox, but after one year transferred to First National, where he was named chief designer. He remained with First National until 1931, after which he opened his own shop and often supplied clothes to studios that did not have a contract designer. In 1935 he joined Bernard Newman on *Roberta,* and when Newman returned to New York, Stevenson was given a contract at RKO that continued for thirteen years. When Howard Hughes bought RKO in 1949, Stevenson moved back to Fox, where he remained until 1951. From 1954 until his death in 1968, he designed Lucille Ball's costumes for her "I Love Lucy" series on television.

Perhaps his best work was done for two films directed by Orson Welles: *Citizen Kane* (1941) and *The Magnificent Ambersons* (1942). His late-nineteenth-century designs for the latter were described by a French film critic as "among the most carefully considered dramatic apparel yet created for an American film."

Walter Plunkett's costumes for Vivien Leigh as Scarlett in Gone With the Wind *perfectly mirrored the changes in the character. We first see her as an innocent and obviously well protected Southern belle, all frills and lightness.*

Plunkett's famed "curtain dress"—the improvised gown Scarlett O'Hara wears on a visit to Rhett Butler with the hope she may enchant him into providing the money to save her beloved Tara. Made from the dining-room portieres by Scarlett's mammy, it remains a masterpiece of ingenuity and Plunkett's best-remembered costume. The short cape and the sash contrived from the curtain's cord and tassels add a touch of dash that suited the spunky Scarlett. The draped hat, trimmed with tail feathers and a claw painted gold (contributed by the last chicken on the plantation before it went into the soup), was designed and made by John Frederics in New York.

The irresistible Vivien Leigh as Scarlett O'Hara. On a shopping spree after her marriage to Rhett Butler, Scarlett indulges herself in countless gowns and fancy hats. This charming dress, with its bodice and apron-front of heavy striped satin, butterfly sleeves edged with pleated organdy, and underskirt of faille banded with a pleated ruffle of the stripe, is pure delight. Miss Leigh's hat was made by John Frederics. The complete outfit is said to have cost $4,000.

Vivien Leigh in Walter Plunkett's garnet-red velvet gown, trimmed with ostrich feathers and paste rubies, one of the most beautiful costumes in Gone With the Wind. *At the star's insistence Plunkett gave her a tulle stole to dispel her fear that the dress made her look too "tarty."*

Bernard Newman is shown here in a studio publicity shot sketching the gowns for RKO's musical Roberta *(1935).*

One of the most famous movie stills in the world is this shot of Judy Garland in Summer Stock *(MGM, 1950). It also reveals Walter Plunkett's wonderful inventiveness. Few designers have dared to dress a star in such a starkly mannish outfit, but the result is nothing less than sensational.*

Ginger Rogers wearing a design by Bernard Newman for RKO's Swing Time *(1936).*

Dolores Del Rio in an Edward Stevenson creation for Journey into Fear *(RKO, 1942).*

Black and white silk bengaline was used by Edward Stevenson for this formal suit Irene Dunne wears in The Joy of Living *(RKO, 1938).*

4

The Forties

REALISM
AND ESCAPISM

THE YEAR 1940 MARKED THE BEGINNING OF A MORE SERIOUS DECADE OF FILM making. With Europe cringing in the shadow of Hitler, and the United States recovering from a depression and apprehensive about involvement in the conflict abroad, movies of the late 1930s and early 1940s began to reflect new concern for the future. John Ford directed the uncompromising and gripping saga *The Grapes of Wrath* (1940) for Fox, for which Gwen Wakeling assembled a wardrobe of ragged and worn clothes that told pointedly of the terrible poverty that a family of westward-bound farmers struggled under. Here was a new kind of costume design for films: faded overalls, hand-me-down calico dresses, battered hats, stained blouses. The pathetic sunbonnet and fraying knitted shawl worn by Jane Darwell as the courageous mother of the Joad family helped, in a measure, to elevate her splendid performance into the realm of truly great cinematic acting.

Even the lithesome Ginger Rogers gave up the chiffon, tulle, and feathers of her dream-dance films with Fred Astaire to wear a white-collared suit designed by Renie (Irene Brouillet Conley), suitable for her role as a secretary in RKO's 1940 *Kitty Foyle,* based on the novel by Christopher Morley. Miss Rogers's performance won her an Academy Award, and Renie's costumes set a new look in the fashion world.

99

And the madcap sprite Carole Lombard turned to more serious endeavors when she appeared in "off the rack" clothes in RKO's 1940 film adaptation of Sidney Howard's stage success *They Knew What They Wanted*. Dressed by Edward Stevenson, Lombard's performance as a waitress who becomes the mail-order wife of Charles Laughton, with near-tragic consequences, revealed a talent for serious drama, far removed from her usual uninhibited movie shenanigans. Of those days of change, Jack Warner would later remark: "All of a sudden, everybody had to begin to act—I mean really *act*—instead of just walk around smiling. And that's when we found out that all a lot of them *could* do was smile."

December 7, 1941, not only marked the entry of the United States into World War II, but signaled the fade-out of Hollywood's most glittering era. The fabled production wonders of the thirties were over. Actresses photographed in soft focus who moved, laughed, pouted, loved (and only rarely died), in dreamlands glowing with floodlit sunshine or klieg moonlight, retreated forever into deepening shadows. Rosie the Riveter, the nurse facing the horrors of Bataan, and the smiling wife controlling her fears for an overseas husband as she fought the war back home were the heroines of the times.

Hollywood's roster of "dreamboat" leading men—Clark Gable, Robert Montgomery, James Stewart, and Robert Taylor—exchanged their well-cut movie apparel for uniforms. Fervidly, Alice Faye, Dorothy Lamour, Judy Garland, and the Brazilian bombshell Carmen Miranda ground out a series of patriotic musicals. Wearing a tight bathing suit and satin pumps, Betty Grable placed a hand on her hip, turned her back, and smiled for a publicity shot that was to become the favorite pin-up photograph of thousands of GIs. Other glamour girls packed a bag, tied their hair in a scarf, and went off to sell war bonds across the country. Carole Lombard died on such a mission in 1942, when her plane crashed into a mountainside. Her grieving husband, Clark Gable, received a telegram from President and Mrs. Roosevelt offering him their sympathy.

Marlene Dietrich donned a Travis Banton–tailored uniform to entertain the troops with songs like "Falling in Love Again" and "Don't Sit Under the Apple Tree with Anyone Else but Me" at training camps, in field hospitals, or on hastily erected plank stages in the jungles of the Pacific. In Hollywood, the gorgeous Marlene joined her glamour-sisters working at the Hollywood Canteen, where she entertained, made immense bowls of her famous potato salad, and washed dishes ("I never broke even one," she later proudly confided).

Though production was hampered by the nation's state of war, making motion pictures went on. Hollywood would soon be selling escape films like *Arabian Nights* (1942) and *White Savage* (1943), both starring Maria Montez. In the tense early months of 1942 the government announced plans to control movie production and restrict the use of raw film stock. A law was passed prohibiting studios from spending more than five thousand dollars on materials to build a new movie set, a restriction that studio technicians managed to circumvent with some skill and ingenuity. Another restriction, which caused considerable anxiety among Hollywood's upper echelon, was one that imposed a ceiling of sixty-seven thousand dollars a year on salaries.

During World War II restrictions on the use of fabric necessarily changed fashions. For a 1944 bond-selling tour, Edith Head designed this cadet blue wool gabardine suit for Dorothy Lamour. The straight, slim skirt and collarless jacket appliquéd with narrow matching binding were accompanied by three changes of crêpe turbans and blouses for variety, in black, white, and scarlet. Head, who had just completed La-mour's wardrobe for The Road to Morocco, *added a touch of star treatment by having each blouse personalized with "Dottie" hand embroidered on a pocket.*

The popularity of today's ubiquitous jeans can be traced back to their introduction by John Wayne and Gary Cooper into westerns of the early forties.

Judy Garland and Mickey Rooney in MGM's Girl Crazy (1943), one of the many musicals in which they starred during the forties.

Copyright 1943 Loew's Incorporated Inc.; renewed 1970 Metro-Goldwyn-Mayer Inc.

Vera West's costume for Maria Montez in Universal's film Cobra Woman (1944). This sort of fantasy-escape was popular with the American public during the tense days of World War II.

Actors, directors, and technicians entered military service: Almost one hundred screen writers were absorbed by the Signal Corps; photographers were in great demand by the Army, Navy, and Air Corps; and the expert workroom personnel, whom designers had depended on to execute their involved designs, turned now to urgent war work that offered them better salaries. Seamstresses stitched parachutes and sewed uniforms, beaders and embroiderers proved adept at the delicate wiring and assembling of numerous vital instruments, and drapers and tailors were recruited to make uniforms for hundreds of thousands of servicemen. Adrian came close to tears when he learned that two patternmakers who for many years had translated his sketches into reality had resigned to head the pattern department of a San Diego firm that manufactured naval-officer uniforms.

The most serious problem faced by a studio designer, however, was the sudden scarcity of luxurious materials needed for the execution of movie costumes. The bugle bead, that minute shimmering bit so indispensable to creating glamorous gowns, was the first to disappear. Before the war such beads were imported in great quantities from Czechoslovakia, but Hitler's annexation of that country had cut off the supply even before America entered the war. Any remaining caches of beads, jet, paste jewels, and sequins were hoarded and guarded jealously by designers, who bartered and traded with rivals for these now-rare commodities.

Fabrics of all kinds became almost impossible to find; the days were gone when fine silk satins and crêpes, metallic lamés, brocades, velvets, and rich weaves could be used with abandon. By 1942 the reserve stocks of fabrics had almost been depleted, and studio workrooms were running under make-do conditions. Used costumes that had been exiled to wardrobe storage racks were remodeled or taken apart and reused, and many of Hollywood's most superb creations were sacrificed to necessity. A skirt from one dinner gown might be used with a top from another and trimmed with the beaded motifs from yet another. Tailored woolens were taken apart, the pieces of fabric redyed and then fashioned into new ensembles. Ribbons, lace edgings, silk flowers, and feathers were used over and over again as trimmings. It was thanks to the cleverness of Hollywood designers that movie costumes continued to have an air of fantasy and extravagance during the lean years of the early forties.

Later, most of the designers would agree that the restrictions and economies enforced in studio wardrobe departments during the war years greatly affected the future of costume design in films. Never again would a film budget tolerate an eleven-yard sable border like the one that enhanced the opera coat Adrian created for Garbo in *Camille,* or exquisite rose-point lace like the wedding veil Hattie Carnegie, the famed New York custom designer, provided Constance Bennett in *Our Betters.* During the war British film studios also had great difficulty with costuming because of similar restrictions and clothing coupons. The English turned to buying clothes from the few custom apparel salons that managed to survive the chaos of bombing and deprivation in London. The wardrobes for women stars were made by Digby Morton, Lachasse, Maison Arthur,

Molyneux, Peter Russell, Victor Stiebel, and Norman Hartnell (who dressed the Queen and the young princesses).

One of the exceptions to the frugality of the war years was the extravagant set of costumes made for Ginger Rogers in Paramount's 1944 screen version of the successful Broadway musical *Lady in the Dark*. Designed by Edith Head, one gown would become a Hollywood fashion classic: a dress fashioned with thirty-five thousand dollars worth of ranch mink skins sewn onto several thicknesses of chiffon so its skirt would move and flow with ease when the actress danced. At one point in her routine Rogers lifted her slit fur skirt to reveal a glittering lining of magenta and gold sequins. (The sequins replaced an earlier lining of bugle beads that was too heavy for one of the movements in the dance.) Another of Miss Rogers' gowns was a wedding dress of such immense proportions it unfortunately inspired giggles rather than awe when the actress appeared wearing it.

The costumes for *Gilda* (Columbia, 1946), which starred Rita Hayworth, were another exception to the austerity of the forties' movie-making world. Jean-Louis, the French-born couturier who began designing for Columbia in 1944, costumed Miss Hayworth with sensuous elegance. He devised gowns of silk tulle enriched by lace insertions and beaded crêpe sheaths that were slit to the knee and above. In *Down to Earth,* made by Columbia in 1947; the sensational red-haired Rita was again garbed by Jean-Louis in a manner befitting her unique love-goddess image.

More representative of the times were serious films put together as quickly as possible on modest budgets. Generally, the clothes for these films were realistic and accessible to women everywhere. The tailored suit (no doubt inspired by the clean, functional lines of military uniforms) became popular, and the simple white or black sheath, made with a minimum of fabric, stayed in fashion and was often made in strapless versions. Extravagant trimming or decoration was, for the most part, absent.

Mrs. Miniver (MGM, 1942), with its moving scenario about war-torn England, starred Greer Garson in simply cut clothes beautifully designed by Robert Kalloch, a designer who had worked for Columbia in the early thirties before joining MGM in 1941. *Casablanca* (Warner Brothers, 1942), another famous film of the period, drew on that faraway exotic city and its background of deadly intrigue for the plot starring Ingrid Bergman and Humphrey Bogart. Wearing Orry-Kelly's deceptively simple costumes, Miss Bergman brought a glowing new image of freshly scrubbed beauty to the screen. Kelly also dressed Bette Davis for her powerful role in *Watch on the Rhine,* Warner Brothers' adaptation of Lillian Hellman's play. As a weary middle-aged woman married to an anti-Nazi German working in the underground, Davis's modest and simple costumes were totally suitable.

The year 1944 saw the release of David O. Selznick's *Since You Went Away,* a film about a representative middle-class American family plunged into bewildering wartime life. The movie's all-star cast included Claudette Colbert, Joseph Cotten, Jennifer Jones, Shirley Temple, and, in a bit part, the former exotic star of the twenties, Nazimova. It was symbolic of the change time had wrought in Hollywood that Colbert, who in 1934 had played Cleopatra in De Mille's lush production, and Nazimova, whose pearl-draped Salome in 1922 had caused a sensation, were now cast in the role of everyday women, stripped of any vestige of glamour.

Hollywood continued to produce new movie stars after the war years, but they were a different breed, less dependent on fabricated allure. Theater marquees now carried the names of Ingrid Bergman, Lauren Bacall, Esther Williams, Van Johnson, Danny Kaye, and a gangly-legged girl with violet eyes named Elizabeth Taylor, who rode to fame in MGM's 1944 *National Velvet*.

By the war's end in 1945, movie audiences were no longer satisfied with the kind of overgarnished fare Hollywood had once served up. In demand were films dealing with serious social problems, subjects that had formerly been taboo in movies. *The Lost Weekend* (Paramount, 1945), a realistic view of alcoholism, brought an Academy Award to its star, Ray Milland. Anti-Semitism, long ignored by Hollywood (where it was rampant), was met head-on in *Gentlemen's Agreement* (Fox, 1947), and the hidden, terrifying institutions inhabited by the mentally ill were revealed in *The Snake Pit* (Fox, 1948), with Olivia de Havilland, who won an Oscar for her performance. In 1949, sparks of the conflagration that would burst between black and white America a decade later lighted movie screens in the form of Stanley Kramer's *Home of the Brave,* Twentieth Century-Fox's *Pinky,* and MGM's *Intruder in the Dust.*

The forties also brought new violence to the screen with tales of horror and murder that were exemplified by three films, all requiring stark, semidocumentary costuming. A fascinating woman urged her lover to push her unconscious husband into the path of an approaching train in Paramount's *Double Indemnity* (1944), a Nazi plot was hatched in *The House on 92nd Street* (Fox, 1945), and a priest was assassinated in *Boomerang* (Fox, 1947).

The rising costs of making films on studio stages (where complicated sets had to be designed and assembled) and steadily rising union wages coupled with demands for increased benefits by set technicians made shooting a movie on location simpler and considerably less expensive. Also, the use of such ready-made settings, complete with the kind of atmosphere demanded by the new realism of scripts that read like police reports, courtroom testimony, or intimate case histories kept by psychiatrists, added to the newsreel look popular in postwar films. Costuming necessarily had to appear as untheatrical as possible, and designers found themselves now asked to "dress her down" when working with a star.

The coming of television, when Americans could turn a dial and bring the entire drama of actual life into their living rooms, certainly had an inestimable effect on motion picture production. Studios spent millions of dollars developing new, wide-screen projectors (CinemaScope, Vistavision, etc.) which they hoped would lessen the effects of the countless home screens that now were kept lighted for hours each day. But though television had a negative impact on the movie industry, millions of people continued to go to the movies regularly for the

Mitchell Leisen (the film's director), Raoul Pene Du Bois, and Edith Head received credit for the costumes in Paramount's film of Kurt Weill's Broadway musical Lady in the Dark (1944). The most famous outfit in the film was this costly gown with its wide skirt, short bolero, and muff all of ranch mink, a relatively rare fur at the time. During her performance of the "Saga of Jenny," Ginger Rogers discarded the fur top and muff and lifted her skirt to perform a dance. Like the bodice, the skirt was lined with glittering arabesque designs of magenta, silver, and gold sequins, and the effect was dazzling. The idea for the gown was Leisen's, and it was designed by Head.

The notorious wedding dress from Lady in the Dark. *Unlike the mink gown, this creation tended to evoke giggles rather than gasps from the audience.*

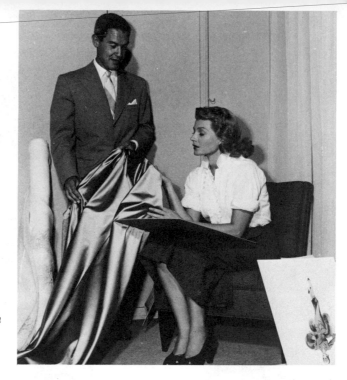

Rita Hayworth consulting with her favorite designer, Jean-Louis.

special kind of pleasure only a movie can offer. Color films and sweeping epics were still the movies' own specialty, something that television with its small screen would never as successfully produce. To this day it is the classic movie spectacles made in Hollywood that are rerun endlessly as Movie Specials on television.

The forties brought proper recognition for movie costume designers when, in 1948, the Motion Picture Academy announced it would henceforth present an Oscar for costume design. Sadly, the Big Three of Hollywood's talented designers had already left the scene. Adrian had resigned in 1942 and was now head of his own immensely successful business. After fourteen years with Paramount, Travis Banton free-lanced for Fox and Universal until 1948. Orry-Kelly had been fired as chief designer at Warner Brothers in 1944, after losing his battle with alcoholism.

The first Academy Award for best costume design for a black-and-white motion picture went to Barbara Karinska for her costuming of Ingrid Bergman in *Joan of Arc* (1948), a highly praised film that turned out to be a financial fiasco. Mme Karinska, a Russian designer who had executed a number of Léon Bakst's designs for Diaghilev's ballets, first came to Hollywood from New York in 1943. Irene, who had replaced Adrian as MGM's chief designer when he resigned the year before, had asked that Karinska be brought to the studio to assist her on Ingrid Bergman's intricate Victorian costumes for *Gaslight*. Karinska's contribution to the film was so successful that she was asked to act again as Irene's aide in creating Marlene Dietrich's Oriental trappings for MGM's 1944 production *Kismet*. After *Kismet* Karinska was one of the designers for Paramount's *Kitty* (1945) and *Unconquered* (1947). She then returned to New York where she ran a highly successful costume house, remaining on the East Coast until she was persuaded to do *Joan of Arc*.

Rita Hayworth, wearing her famous Jean-Louis black satin gown in Columbia's 1946 film Gilda. Jean-Louis handled the slippery satin so that it became an integral part of Hayworth as she sang and danced "Put the Blame on Mame, Boys." In this number the costume, the song, and the character met in perfect fusion—and the influence on Hollywood musicals was historic.

Hayworth in another gorgeous Jean-Louis costume from Gilda.

In 1948 the category of best costume designer was added to the roster of awards given yearly by the Academy of Motion Picture Arts and Sciences. The first recipient of this Oscar was Barbara Karinska, the distinguished stage costumer who had been brought to Hollywood by RKO to dress Ingrid Bergman for Joan of Arc. Mme Karinska's artistry suited Bergman's luminous performance, and her costumes, made from hand-loomed copies of fabrics researched in museums, totally sewn by hand and cut and constructed exactly in the manner of the fifteenth century, set new standards for period-costume design for films. Deceptively simple, they have seldom (if ever) been equaled for authenticity.

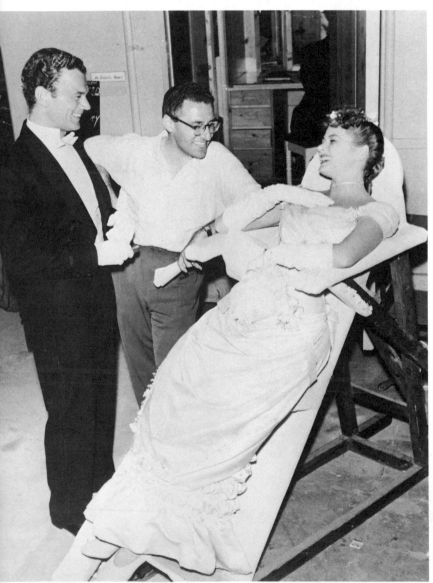

Ingrid Bergman (on leaning board) between takes of MGM's Gaslight (1944). She is talking with co-star Joseph Cotten and director George Cukor. Barbara Karinska assisted Irene with the intricate Victorian costumes for this film.

The designer who met what was perhaps the greatest challenge of the late forties and early fifties was Edith Head at Paramount. Head was called on to costume Gloria Swanson for her return to the screen in the role of an ego-consumed has-been movie queen on the verge of madness. Stories about director Billy Wilder's acid-etched Gothic Hollywood tale abound. It is said that the script of *Sunset Boulevard* was first sent to the recluse chatelaine of Pickfair, Mary Pickford, who rejected it with the warning that the film would destroy Hollywood's image forever. Then, Barbara Stanwyck sent it back to Wilder with "No!" scrawled across the title page, stating the film would ruin any actress unwise enough to accept the part. Joan Crawford, Bette Davis, and Miriam Hopkins are also said to have turned down the role before the film's producers had the inspiration of showing it to Gloria Swanson.

Long absent from movie screens, Swanson had embarked on a career playing drawing-room comedies on the stage and must have realized the public would see unflattering parallels between the character of Norma Desmond, the faded movie actress, and her own life. And, the money she would receive (fifty-thousand dollars for five weeks' work) was minute compared with the salary she had once commanded as Paramount's "Glorious Gloria." But the role of Norma Desmond fascinated Swanson, and she could sense what the other actresses had not discerned: It was a true star role in a melodrama that had the potential of making motion picture history. More than the tragedy of a deranged movie star caught in the web of her past glory, *Sunset Boulevard* revealed for the first time the peculiar contents of the film industry's carefully guarded closets. After reading its powerful scenario, one of Paramount's executives had stated: "It's suicide! It will destroy the special thing movies have come to symbolize to the world."

Accustomed to the ranting of front-office executives predicting ruin, Swanson signed to do the film, and one of her first requests was that Edith Head be costume designer. When news got out at the Paramount studios that Swanson was returning, a long-time wardrobe employee recalled that it seemed "like the old days . . . at last someone got around to repainting the fitting room."

Together, Head and Swanson worked out the problems of costuming a still-beautiful actress as a faded and forgotten movie star. Head prepared and discarded sketches, and the two women considered and rejected countless bolts of fabric, shoes, accessories, and jewelry, analyzing both their dramatic and photographic qualities. "We were co-designers," Head would later comment. Swanson, who, for a time, had managed her own New York dress-manufacturing firm and had designed its lines, was well equipped to work with Head assembling her comeback wardrobe. The result of the collaboration was a tour de force of movie costuming. Norma Desmond had a look of grandeur that was peculiarly out of place in a changed world. Though she wore contemporary clothes, they had touches reminiscent of the Hollywood of silent movies. Shades

Gloria Swanson on the set of Paramount's Sunset Boulevard *(1950).*

Miss Swanson was reunited with Cecil B. De Mille, one of her first directors, for Sunset Boulevard. *Swanson plays Norma Desmond, an aging film star, and De Mille appears as himself. (*Sunset Boulevard *© MCMLII by Paramount Pictures Corporation. All rights reserved)*

Gloria Swanson wearing two of Edith Head's costumes for Sunset Boulevard.

of the young Adrian, Howard Greer, and Travis Banton followed Swanson as she moved through the vast empty halls and rooms of her pseudo–Italian palazzo, its garden choked with weeds, the drained swimming pool a playground for scurrying rats.

The fact that *Sunset Boulevard* was shot in black-and-white rather than in color enhanced the film's nostalgic quality. The fabrics used for Swanson's wardrobe—chiffon, velvet, tulle, brocade, taffeta, leopard-printed crêpe—were used in a discordant manner. The printed crêpe was draped into a poolside ensemble that might have served for an Eastern courtesan in a De Mille epic. Black velvet was used for an afternoon tailleur, unexpectedly trimmed with white ermine; black tulle fashioned a sweeping negligée that echoed the ghost of Mae Murray and subtly communicated the wearer's preoccupation with a time when movie stars wore costumes off as well as on the screen.

Extravagant fur trimming was used to give an air of the forgotten movie queen's royal past. There was a brocaded gown worn with an outmoded shoulder wrap of gray chinchilla; the black velvet suit Norma Desmond wore on her triumphant (she believed) return to the Paramount lot featured lapels, a toque hat, and a small barrel muff of white ermine; a white crêpe evening gown was worn under a cape of the same fabric, lavishly bordered with bands of white fox à la Pola Negri.

Sunset Boulevard premiered at Radio City Music Hall in New York on August 10, 1950. It was pronounced a smash hit, the *New York Times* critic noting that it was "inconceivable that anyone else might have been considered for the role of Norma Desmond." Swanson received her third nomination for an Academy Award, but the Oscar went to Judy Holliday for *Born Yesterday.* Although Head's costumes for *Sunset Boulevard* were also bypassed by the Academy, Head did receive two awards that year: for *All About Eve,* in the category of black-and-white film (Twentieth Century-Fox, shared with Charles LeMaire), and for *Samson and Delilah,* in the category of best costume design for a color film (Paramount, shared with Dorothy Jeakins, Elois Jenssen, Gile Steele, and Gwen Wakeling).

Twenty-four years later, in 1974, Gloria Swanson again returned to Paramount as the narrator of a television documentary concerning the studio's greatest movies. For the film, Swanson asked to wear a remake of the black-velvet-and-white-ermine suit Edith Head had designed for her as Norma Desmond. Not only had the ensemble vanished, but not one white peacock feather could be found to decorate the new ermine toque made for her. Swanson was aghast. "Imagine," she said, "not one single white peacock feather in all Hollywood!" Clearly Hollywood had changed, and one of Norma Desmond's lines from the film summed it up well: "I'm still big—it's the pictures that have grown small!"

INNOVATIONS AND A DWINDLING BOX OFFICE

DURING THE FIFTIES, HOLLYWOOD MOVIEMAKERS SUPPLIED AUDIENCES with a generous number of attractive, successful films that perfectly suited the quiet exuberance of the secure Eisenhower years. The 1948 court decision that movie corporations could not own their own theaters (thus taking away exclusive distribution of their properties) led to each film's being sold on the basis of its individual potential. The rise of the director began when distributors no longer looked to a film's star for box-office success, but rather sought movies that were directed by highly professional top men who knew how to put together a sure-fire smash hit (not just build vehicles to frame a special star). Only a few, rare stars survived, like the determined Elizabeth Taylor.

It was Twentieth Century-Fox who found what was possibly the last great star in the old tradition: the incomparable Marilyn Monroe. She first stirred audiences and alerted producers to her potential when she played a brief role in Fox's 1950 sophisticated comedy *All About Eve,* concerning love and hate among New York's theater circle. Written and directed by Joseph Mankiewicz, with a superb cast that was headed by Bette Davis in the role of Margo Channing (said to be modeled after Tallulah Bankhead), everything about the film worked, including the costumes. Edith Head dressed Miss Davis, at the star's request, and the other wardrobes were the responsibility of Charles LeMaire.

Marilyn Monroe, photographed by Cecil Beaton.

Head shared an Academy Award for best costumes with LeMaire—who, in truth, had actually done very little on the film. But it was the unveiling of the innocent beauty of the breathless Marilyn that brought a touch of genuine Hollywood magic back to the screen.

By 1953 Twentieth Century-Fox realized that Marilyn Monroe was on the verge of stardom and cast her as the "Little Girl from Little Rock" with a connoisseur's respect for diamonds: Lorelei Lee, the most famous heroine of the twenties, from Anita Loos' *Gentlemen Prefer Blondes*. Wearing costumes by William Travilla, Marilyn delighted audiences with her antics on an international treasure hunt.

William Travilla had designed costumes at Columbia Pictures from 1941 to 1943, then transferred to Warner Brothers, where he remained from 1946 until 1949. He then signed with Twentieth Century-Fox, where, except for an occasional free-lance film, he remained from 1950 to 1958. Often understated but always complimentary, Travilla's designs for Monroe suited her spontaneous freshness. Travis Banton had once remarked that Carole Lombard wore her clothes "like perfume . . . she could just sort of splash them on and forget about them." The same was true with Monroe. Her loosely brushed hair, makeup that seemed unstudied, and constant effervescence made hers the most highly individualistic screen image to be seen in decades. Among other films which reflect some of Travilla's best work for her are *Monkey Business* (1952), *How to Marry a Millionaire* (1953), *There's No Business Like Show Business* (1954), and *Bus Stop* (1956).

A scene from All About Eve *(Twentieth Century-Fox, 1950), in which the young Marilyn Monroe played a small part. Edith Head and Charles LeMaire shared an Academy Award for costume design for this film.*

Marilyn in a scene from Gentlemen Prefer Blondes *(Twentieth Century-Fox, 1953). William Travilla designed Marilyn's costumes and Charles LeMaire was responsible for all the other costumes in this production.*

The 1954 production of There's No Business Like Show Business *starred Marilyn Monroe in costumes designed by William Travilla.*

Movie stars of the 1950s formed another constellation. Postwar fans opened their hearts to the sort of girl one could find in a station wagon parked at a suburban railroad station waiting for the 6:22 to bring home her tennis-tanned junior-executive husband. Neatly dressed to complement her Brooks Brothers–garbed mate, her hair naturally coiffed and her face only lightly touched with makeup, this cool, well-mannered woman who mothered nearly perfect children had the secure charm of a Bryn Mawr alumna. At home were jars brimming with cookies, a drawing room filled with French provincial furniture, a shaggy dog romping across a green-carpet lawn, and an adored domestic busy in a kitchen hung with copper pots and pans. America was well and happy and this kind of woman typified Hollywood's idea of what every woman aspired to be.

Youngsters like Elizabeth Taylor, Debbie Reynolds, and Jane Powell had grown into sweet womanhood, and Doris Day was about to have *her* day—one that would last seemingly interminably. More serious roles went to neatly sultry types like Susan Hayward, Deborah Kerr, and Lana Turner. A look of expensive good taste combined with simple allure marked the movie clothes of stars during these years, and the two movie designers who most largely contributed to this neat-as-a-pin, department-store better-dresses fashion mystique were Helen Rose at MGM and Edith Head at Paramount.

During her long tenure at MGM, Helen Rose costumed almost every major actress who made films there. During the fifties she dressed Elizabeth Taylor for *Father of the Bride* (1950), in which she gave Miss Taylor a wedding gown that was widely copied by New York manufacturers. The year 1952 saw Rose costuming Lana Turner for two of her greatest successes: *The Merry Widow* and *The Bad and the Beautiful* (for which Rose received an Academy Award for best costumes in a black-and-white film). In 1955, Rose costumed Esther Williams for *Jupiter's Darling;* in 1956, *The Swan,* with Grace Kelly; *Cat on a Hot Tin Roof,* in 1958, with a more sophisticated Elizabeth Taylor. As "Maggie the cat" in Tennesee Williams' drama set in the modern South, Miss Taylor appeared wearing only three costumes, a slip, a simple blouse and skirt, and a white chiffon gown with a revealing décolletage.

The chiffon gown caused a sensation and is still possibly the most beautiful dress Taylor ever appeared in on the screen. The star asked Rose to make it up for her personal wardrobe, and Rose received so many requests for copies of the dress that she decided to enter the wholesale garment business, a venture that proved highly successful.

At Paramount, Edith Head did outstanding work for Audrey Hepburn in *Roman Holiday* (1953, for which both Hepburn and Head were awarded Oscars), and *Sabrina* (1954, again an Academy winner for Head). In 1955, Head costumed Grace Kelly in *To Catch a Thief,* the film the designer has said is her own personal favorite of the many costume jobs she has done over the years. The amazing Miss Head received nominations for the Academy Award for every year of the 1950s. Among them: 1956, *The Proud and the Profane;* 1958, *The Buccaneer;* 1959, *Career* (black-and-white) and *The Five Pennies* (color).

Such constant recognition of Miss Head's talents would continue into the 1960s when, except for 1967 and 1968, her name would appear every year among the nominees for best costume design. What has made her work so exceptional is her innate recognition of the points about an actress that might best be highlighted and those that were best left alone, and her ability to gain a star's trust and thus her cooperation in dressing her. This has made for a smooth, compatible operation that expressed itself in clothes that seemed a natural, integral part of both the actress and her performance. Head's famous remark, "If I had sketched a gown with a square neckline and a star wanted a round one instead, I let her have it. I never argued with her," fairly well sums up her working technique with the many varied temperaments with which she has had to cope.

Elizabeth Taylor and Spencer Tracy in MGM's 1950 production of Father of the Bride. Costume design for this film was by Helen Rose.

Helen Rose received an Academy Award for costuming Lana Turner in MGM's The Bad and the Beautiful (1952).

In MGM's 1952 production of The Merry Widow, Lana Turner wears this gown designed by Helen Rose; it is made of black Lyons velvet trimmed with jet embroidered hand-run Alençon lace. Miss Turner was so fond of this gown that she asked the designer to adapt it for her personal wardrobe.

Sheer lace, satin Lastex, and jeweled straps adorn this bathing suit worn by Esther Williams in Million Dollar Mermaid (MGM, 1950). Miss Rose's designs for the actress influenced such bathing suit manufacturers as Catalina, Jantzen, and Rose Marie Reid to find new, lighter fabrics. They eagerly awaited every movie Esther Williams made, for they would copy the innovative designs for the American public, turning bathing suits into big business.

In a quintessential moment from Cat on a Hot Tin Roof (MGM, 1958), Elizabeth Taylor as "Maggie the Cat" appeared in this Helen Rose design, one of the three costumes she wears throughout the film.

A strong influence of French couture was another phenomenon of fifties movie fashion. The instances are numerous: Christian Dior, who had designed successfully for French films, costumed Jennifer Jones in David Selznick's 1954 production of *The Indiscretion of an American Wife* (for which he was nominated for an Academy Award), and Olivia de Havilland in 1956's *The Ambassador's Daughter*. Dior's first American film assignment had come when he dressed Marlene Dietrich (a bit too flamboyantly, perhaps) for Alfred Hitchcock's *Stage Fright* (1950); until 1957 he designed for movies with some degree of frequency.

Hubert de Givenchy made his Hollywood debut as Edith Head's codesigner for Paramount's 1957 Audrey Hepburn–Fred Astaire musical *Funny Face,* for which they shared an Academy Award nomination. In 1961 he joined forces with Head and the New York designer Pauline Trigère to again dress Miss Hepburn, in *Breakfast at Tiffany's*. In 1963 he co-designed, with Pierre Cardin, Elizabeth Taylor's wardrobe for *The VIPs*.

Edith Head won her fifth Academy Award for her designs for Roman Holiday *(Paramount, 1953), starring Audrey Hepburn.*

Elizabeth Taylor in a dress Edith Head designed for her appearance in Elephant Walk *(Paramount, 1954).*

Schiaparelli, who between 1934 and 1938 had been credited as designer for eight films, turned her talents to the screen once again in 1952, when she and the French illustrator-designer Marcel Vertès designed the costumes for *Moulin Rouge.* Pierre Balmain dressed Lana Turner in *Betrayed* (1954), Rita Hayworth in *Fire Down Below* (1957), and Cyd Charisse in *Two Weeks in Another Town* (1962). Balmain was also responsible for Sophia Loren's extravagant wardrobe in *The Millionairess* (1960).

Over the years, English film makers have frequently availed themselves of the services of English couturiers. Norman Hartnell, Charles Creed, Digby Morton, Molyneux, and, more recently, Mary Quant have all designed for the movies. For the 1966 production *Two for the Road,* Audrey Hepburn temporarily abandoned Givenchy to have her wardrobe designed by an assortment of couturiers, including: Mary Quant, Michèle Rosier, Paco Rabanne, Foale & Tuffin, and Ken Scott. Clare Rendelsham was credited as costume supervisor.

But the strongest trend of the fifties, as far as movie fashion is concerned, was toward big-budget musicals. Among them, *An American in Paris,* starring Gene Kelly and Leslie Caron, was outstanding. Although Walter Plunkett and Orry-Kelly designed many of the film's costumes, Irene Sharaff, with her ballet scene set on the streets of Paris, stole the show. Her expertise in designing both costumes and décor for this memorable sequence brought new visual excitement to the screen and firmly established her as a designer of exceptional talent. Her unique gift for costuming ballet was obvious, as was her ability to create a series of eclectic backgrounds inspired by the streets of Paris. Countless dance garments were made, some suggesting figures from the paintings of Lautrec, Degas, and other French painters. Possessing an extraordinary sense of color and an innate flair for the dramatic, Sharaff's ballet costumes must surely rank among the most effective ever designed for the screen. Her choice of fabrics, insistence on authentic shape, and flawless construction made the Parisian ballet not only the highlight of *An American in Paris,* but perhaps the most successfully designed dance ever created for a film. Though she shared the 1951 Academy Award for best costume design for a color film with Orry-Kelly and Walter Plunkett, it was Irene Sharaff who truly carried off the honor.

In 1952, Franz Lehar's waltz phenomenon *The Merry Widow* was revived for the third time by MGM. It was a sumptuous production built around the talents of Lana Turner, with Fernando Lamas in the role of the dashing Prince Danilo. Miss Turner, as the sophisticated widow, was gowned by Helen Rose, without, perhaps, too much fidelity to the script's period, but certainly with the kind of slick elegance Miss Rose was admirably noted for. For the famous waltz scene, Turner wore a fitted black velvet gown that flared above the knees, richly embroidered with black jet. Black egret feathers clasped to her light blond hair added the required touch of Viennese schmaltz. Rose's designs were highly publicized, and a version of the waltz dress (see page 123) was made for Miss Turner's personal wardrobe (with practically no alteration whatever of the original "period" costume).

The year 1953 saw three of Broadway's smash-hit musicals brought to the screen: Cole Porter's *Kiss Me Kate* (MGM), wittily costumed by Walter Plunkett; Irving Berlin's *Call Me Madam* (Fox), again showing the deft touch of Irene Sharaff; and MGM's *The Band Wagon,* with music by Howard Dietz and Arthur Schwartz, costumed by Mary Ann Nyberg, a free-lance designer active during the mid-fifties. Nyberg was with MGM in 1953, then designed briefly for Fox (*Carmen Jones,* 1954) and for Warner Brothers (*A Star Is Born,* 1954) until 1955, when she retired.

Twentieth Century-Fox, with Magna, drew from the New York theater in 1955 when it acquired the rights to produce *Oklahoma!,* Richard Rodgers and Oscar Hammerstein's adaptation of Lynn Riggs' Theatre Guild-success *Green*

Grow the Lilacs, which had changed the entire format of the American musical theater. Orry-Kelly was signed on a free-lance basis to create the costumes for the film and Broadway's leading scenic designer, Oliver Smith, was named production designer. Making the film, Smith recalls, was "one of the happiest working experiences I have ever known. At that time, Fox was still one of the last studios that was doing things in a big way. It was the answer to a designer's dream. We were paid very well, lived in style, and had the superb technical facilities of the studio's scenic departments at our disposal. The prop men and scenic artists were unequalled—there was nothing they couldn't achieve and money was the least of our problems. It was artistic bliss."

Oklahoma! unfolded on windswept plains and featured box-lunch picnics and foot-stomping dances choreographed by Agnes De Mille. Orry-Kelly's costumes of calico, denim, loomed homespuns, and crocheted lace perfectly suited the American-primitive look of the film and were a great asset to Arthur Hornblow's production. Wearing a sunbonnet and ruffles, Shirley Jones epitomized the new kind of self-reliant heroine that she repeated in Rodgers and Hammerstein's *Carousel* a year later. *Oklahoma!* was as refreshing as a swallow of cold water from a tin dipper and left audiences with a taste for more such uncomplicated, home-grown entertainment.

Rodgers and Hammerstein provided the source for another highly spectacular film musical: In 1956, Twentieth Century-Fox produced their Siamese delight, *The King and I,* with the glossy-domed Yul Brynner making his film debut and Deborah Kerr cast in the role played on the stage by the exquisite Gertrude Lawrence. Irene Sharaff was called on as costume designer. She used magnificent Thai silks (discovered in a small import shop hidden away in New York's East Sixties) lavished with gold embroidery and jewels for Brynner's royal raiment. For the wide-hooped gowns worn by Miss Kerr as the proper English school teacher, she selected simpler fabrics. The resulting contrast was an Academy Award-winning combination that year. Sharaff's designs also included a group of magnificent ballet costumes, ones that rivaled her creations in *An American In Paris* for originality and charm.

Over the years, few foreign designers actually worked in Hollywood, but none was more successful when he did than the late Sir Cecil Beaton. Though Beaton had had an active career designing for English films (between 1941 and 1947 he was credited for nine films produced in England), his Hollywood debut came in 1958 when he was invited to create both décor and costumes for MGM's *Gigi,* a movie musical adapted by Alan Jay Lerner and Frederick Loewe from a story by Colette. Vincente Minnelli, the director, made an inspired choice in Beaton, who had already proved his talents with the sensational late-Edwardian costumes he had created for the stage version of Lerner and Loewe's brilliant musical *My Fair Lady*. An internationally famed photographer and author of countless books on fashion and manners, the tall, elegantly dressed Englishman was a personal friend of Colette and had paid frequent visits to her Palais Royal apartment in Paris to photograph her. There amidst the disarray he

When Marlene Dietrich appeared in Warner Brothers' 1950 Stage Fright *she went to Christian Dior in Paris for her "new look" wardrobe. This gown of chiffon with self-covered belt, draped bodice, and handmade self-fabric flowers, is worn with the kind of hat Dior made popular. Miss Dietrich's necklace and bracelets are of diamonds and emeralds, and were borrowed from Cartier for the film. Lovely as she looked, one is conscious of a certain overdressing and a lack of the cool, serene mystery Travis Banton had given her years earlier.*

Dietrich would later appear more elegantly costumed by the French-born de-signer Jean-Louis in The Monte Carlo Story *(United Artists, 1957).*

130

Two Weeks in Another Town *(MGM, 1962) starred Cyd Charisse in costumes by Pierre Balmain.*

Irene Sharaff won special praise (and shared an Oscar) for her ballet costumes worn by Gene Kelly and Leslie Caron dancing in the Parisian streets in An American In Paris (MGM, 1951).

Orry-Kelly's costumes, Agnes De Mille's choreography, and stars Shirley Jones and Gordon MacRae made Oklahoma! a smashing success for Twentieth Century-Fox/Magna in 1956.

Drawing on brilliant Thai silks and jewels to dress Yul Brynner and elegant, full-skirted designs for Deborah Kerr, Irene Sharaff created an unforgettable Academy Award–winning wardrobe for The King and I *(1956). Brynner, as the male-chauvinistic King of Siam, is raving about the superiority of his sex, but will be delighted shortly when Miss Kerr, as an English governess, shows him what a vigorous polka can do to further his appreciation of her own country's customs.*

Miss Kerr's magnificent dance gown, fashioned from the heaviest satin and draped over a heavy hoop frame, caused the actress to complain—until she saw herself in the day's rushes, moving like a great shimmering tulip across the mirrorlike palace floor. Sharaff's costume was not only appropriate for the scene, it made it a thrilling spectacle.

Cecil Beaton was one of those rare designers capable of creating both the costumes and sets for a film, a talent
he demonstrated admirably in MGM's production of Lerner and Loewe's Gigi (1958). Here, Leslie Caron
and Isobel Elsom are pictured in the fussy, overdressed world of Paris during the late nineteenth century. For
his efforts Beaton received an Academy Award.

had found her "propped up on pillows and cushions and covered with mountains of rugs and hot water bottles, with her marvelous powdered face, grey frizzy hair, and dark painted eyes."

Late-nineteenth-century splendor was the background for several unforgettable costume displays in the film. The glittering evening at Maxim's required Beaton to design twenty ensembles for the haughty ladies of the demimonde who moved through the famed art nouveau–decorated restaurant like a flock of heavily jeweled birds, wearing gowns of violet satin, garnet velvet, lemon silk, emerald brocade—lavished with lace, clusters of silk flowers, rich embroidery, and fountains of egret and bird-of-paradise plumage. For sheer sumptuousness, the mise-en-scène is resplendent. A scene at the film's end, set in the sun-dappled Bois de Boulogne in the spring, called for 150 costumes of an extraordinary variety: fashionable women on horseback, jaunty military officers, children at play attended by their nursemaids, jet-covered dowagers observing the promenade from behind lorgnettes, femmes fatales slinking along in hobble skirts, boulevardiers swinging their gold-headed canes, shop girls in their modest holiday-best frocks, cut like those in a Renoir painting. Amidst the flurry of nineteenth-century Parisians parading under the broad trees, Leslie Caron, like a delicate hothouse bloom, created a sensation in a sheath of pale lilac-colored ribbon lace and an audacious bonnet trimmed with ostrich tips and branches of egret. It is not surprising that Beaton was chosen as the recipient of 1958's Academy Award for best costume design for a color film.

6

The Sixties
and Seventies

THE
RISE OF THE
INDEPENDENTS

DURING THE 1960's, NEW PRODUCTION TECHNIQUES CONTINUED TO APPEAR. Indeed, as Norma Desmond had cried in *Sunset Boulevard* a decade earlier, "The pictures have grown small." Budgets assumed major importance and the costume departments were one of the first places that expenses were cut. More and more films were made on location instead of designing and constructing costly sets, crews were trimmed to the bone, and only a shadow of the troupe of technicians formerly needed for filming was maintained. The growing demand for utter realism required costumes that had a straight-from-the-rack look; indeed, countless films were so costumed, with a designer acting more as a "shopper" for suitable garments than as an artist who was an integral part of a carefully conceived production. The making of films was no longer confined to Hollywood. New York City, Mexico, Italy, Yugoslavia, London all became popular (and far less expensive) locations for Americans to work on. And, too, there was the growing impact of television with its new roster of stars (Lucille Ball became America's new slapstick sweetheart) to be dealt with. "All the fun went out of making movies," veteran star Mary Astor remarked; "they turned out pictures like waffles."

Two outstanding costume films of the 1960s were *West Side Story* (1961) and *Cleopatra* (1963), which was possibly the last unabashed "epic" to be built

When the Broadway musical West Side Story *was brought to the screen in 1961, Irene Sharaff repeated her job as costume designer. Jerome Robbins served as choreographer, and his extraordinary ballet sequences demanded costumes that could withstand the vigorous movements he required, look like authentic New York street-gang garb, and still achieve a degree of visual artistry. Sharaff succeeded admirably in filling all these requirements, and though the clothes worn by the "Sharks" and the "Jets" appeared genuine, they were in truth constructed of special fabric. The blue jeans for the boys, for instance, were made from a denim specially woven with an elastic thread, dyed, bleached, redyed, and "distressed" to appear worn and aged, all at great expense and with great effort.*

around a star—in this instance, Elizabeth Taylor. Both movies had Irene Sharaff as costume designer, and for *West Side Story* she added another Oscar to her growing collection. Sharaff attained a high degree of convincing realism in her designs for this modern-dress version of *Romeo and Juliet*, set in New York's Puerto Rican barrio, and she did so without sacrificing an ensemble quality that distinguished them for their originality and beauty—a difficult and notable achievement. In spite of the garments' utterly ordinary appearance, Sharaff insisted all major costumes be made from her painted sketches, with great care given to aging and "distressing" them to look authentic. The movie contained large sequences of ballet, and here Sharaff's understanding of what a ballet costume must be once again resulted in dance garments that not only looked totally convincing but allowed the dancers total freedom to perform the vigorous choreography required of them.

Twentieth Century-Fox's 1963 version of the standard star vehicle—again the story of Egypt's Serpent of the Nile, Cleopatra—was selected as a showcase for the still ravishing Elizabeth Taylor. The role had been played by Theda Bara in 1917, Claudette Colbert in 1934, Vivien Leigh in 1946, and Rhonda Fleming in 1952, but Fox announced that this production, adorned with the full-blooming charms of Miss Taylor, would knock 'em dead! Instead, it was Twentieth Century-Fox that almost expired under the top-heavy production cost, one that finally totalled over forty million dollars. From the first the production was plagued with financial problems that became so chaotic the very foundations of the studio shook dangerously.

A major cost setback was the complete replacement of a set of elaborate costumes designed by Oliver Messel. No doubt Messel's very excellent dressing of Vivien Leigh in a 1945 English-made adaptation of George Bernard Shaw's *Caesar and Cleopatra*, seemed to qualify him for Fox's production, but disagreements between star and producers developed, and while the company was on location in Rome, where they were to begin shooting, Messel was replaced by Irene Sharaff.

Working frantically against a tight production schedule, Miss Sharaff based her designs on historical sources—ancient sculptures, wall paintings, and museum treasures. She costumed Taylor in a series of thirty-four perfectly cut and proportioned, often severe, fitted gowns. Made of supple fabrics, they were gorgeously decorated with superb reproductions of authentic Egyptian jewelry and rich trimmings of jewel-set gold embroidery. The headpieces Sharaff had made for the star were unsurpassed in their authenticity and beauty, and the 1963 Academy Award for best costume design for a color film she shared with Vittorio Nino Novarese and Renie was well deserved.

But the great movie-event of the decade came in 1964. When *My Fair Lady* opened on Broadway in 1956, wily Jack Warner acquired the film rights to Lerner and Loewe's wonderful musical adaptation of Shaw's *Pygmalion* for a reputed sum of five million dollars—said to be the largest amount ever paid for a theatrical property up to that time. Warner's foresight would pay off admirably.

A HEROINE
  WHO HAS PROVIDED
    RICH MOVIE FARE FOR DECADES—
          CLEOPATRA

The first screen Cleopatra was Theda Bara in Famous Players-Lasky's 1917 Edwardian version of life in ancient Egypt. An unknown costume designer lavished Miss Bara with peacock feathers in a way that would never be equaled.

Travis Banton gave Claudette Colbert's Cleopatra this heavy jeweled collar, capturing the stateliness of the ancient Egyptian kingdom (Paramount, 1934).

Another Cleopatra, as portrayed by Vivien Leigh in Gabriel Pascal's elaborate 1946 version of Shaw's Caesar and Cleopatra. *Oliver Messel, the immensely talented English theater designer, costumed Pascal's production with daring and magnificence.*

In 1963, Elizabeth Taylor as a sultry Cleopatra was given a set of suitably gorgeous and expensive costumes designed by Irene Sharaff. This exquisite headdress, executed to a Fabergé-like perfection, is a tribute to Miss Sharaff's skill in adapting her extensive research into the period to her designs. Albeit a financial disaster, the film stands beside the Cleopatras of Travis Banton and Oliver Messel for its conception of Egypt's most cinematic heroine.

Later, after almost eighteen months of work, and at an expenditure of more than fourteen million dollars, *My Fair Lady* opened in 1964, with Audrey Hepburn and Rex Harrison in the starring roles. At once it was a sellout and a catalyst for the same kind of box-office fever that the stage production had caused on Broadway. Cecil Beaton received two Academy Awards for his efforts: one for best costume design for a color motion picture, and a second Oscar for best art direction.

The job had been a Herculean one. For months Beaton had painted endless costume sketches and had worked simultaneously with George Cukor, the film's director, touring London to find and photograph the locations that were eventually reproduced in Warner Brothers' Burbank studios. Covent Garden and its markets, an Edwardian pub, and the house on Wimpole Street (once occupied by Beaton's family doctor) that served as the model for Professor Higgins' bachelor lodgings were photographed and noted with the care of archaeologists recording ancient relics. For the art nouveau house of the professor's mother, Beaton turned for inspiration to the late Victorian illustrations of Kate Greenaway and Walter Crane.

By the time he reached Hollywood, Beaton was armed with several portfolios of sketches and volumes of research. He then searched antique shops (as well as junk and thrift shops) in Los Angeles and San Francisco for washstands, Oriental objets d'art, old gramophones, letter racks, door knobs and hinges, bathroom fittings, even a cigar box for Higgins' study. The wallpapers for the interiors were adapted from original designs by William Morris, England's leading exponent of art nouveau in the early 1900s, and were faithfully printed in London especially for the production. Carpets and upholstery fabrics of the period were woven to order.

The film also required many more costumes than had the stage version. In the famous black-and-white Ascot scene there were over a hundred carefully selected women extras (compared with only twenty in the play), all gowned in brilliant re-creations of Edwardian fashions. It was Edwardian style at an haute couture level, with echoes of Poiret and Lucile. A perfectionist, the designer personally checked the makeup and hairstyles as well as every ruffle and ribbon to make sure his creations were flawless. The hats worn in this scene were so immense that an army surplus tin quonset hut was erected on the Warner Brothers lot to serve as a dressing room. To capture the special posture peculiar to the period, the actresses were required to hold balletlike stances, which Beaton himself demonstrated.

Beaton has written that true achievement in theater should "shower the spectator with illusions not to be found at home." *My Fair Lady* was a bouquet of assorted rare illusions he offered to the movies. It is doubtful whether moviegoers will ever again be proffered such an exquisite gift.

Rodgers and Hammerstein were again represented on the screen when, in 1965, Warner Brothers produced their immensely successful Broadway musical about the singing Trapp family of Austria, *The Sound of Music*. Filmed on location in Austria, the film starred Julie Andrews, wearing a set of charming

The 1913 drawing of Paul Poiret's lampshade-tunicked gown that Cecil Beaton adapted for one of the extras in the famed Ascot scene of Warner Brothers' 1964 My Fair Lady.

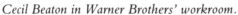

Cecil Beaton in Warner Brothers' workroom.

Tyrolean costumes designed by Dorothy Jeakins. Miss Jeakins, who had been a sketch artist for Twentieth Century-Fox in 1938, returned to that studio for three years in the early fifties. And in 1958 she had been responsible for the wardrobe in another Rodgers-Hammerstein opus, *South Pacific*—which she had also costumed on Broadway. Jeakins dressed Marilyn Monroe for *Let's Make Love* (United Artists, 1961) and more recently costumed Universal's 1975 disaster-epic, *The Hindenburg*, which starred Anne Bancroft. For her costumes in *The Sound of Music*, Jeakins was nominated for the 1965 Academy Award for best design for a color film.

Audrey Hepburn wearing the gown Cecil Beaton adapted from Poiret. Though Beaton has in essence kept to Poiret's original, his own witty sense of chic comes through in the towering be-plumed hat. The stylized roses have become abstract circles. Miss Hepburn was so delighted when she saw this gown that though it was not designed for her she begged to be allowed to model it for Beaton's camera. (Photograph by Cecil Beaton)

Audrey Hepburn in the famous Ascot dress designed by Beaton for My Fair Lady. *(Photograph by Cecil Beaton)*

Cecil Beaton holds high one of the hats he designed for the Ascot scene, while Leah Barnes, Warner Brothers' chief milliner, models another.

Unfortunately, however, the film musical in general was fast becoming a thing of the past. Most such expensive ventures lost money, including Lerner and Loewe's Arthurian romance, *Camelot* (1967). The successful Broadway production had featured costumes by Adrian (and Tony Duquette)—Adrian's last assignment. Warner Brothers signed John Truscott to create the large number of designs needed for the huge cast headed by Richard Harris and Vanessa Redgrave. An excellent free-lance designer, Truscott had costumed Lerner and Loewe's Paramount adaptation of their stage success *Paint Your Wagon* in 1969. Though that film had been a financial disaster, Truscott's costumes were highly original and earned him critical praise. A perfectionist, Truscott's fairy-tale designs for *Camelot* stand among the most exceptional period-movie costumes of the sixties.

Turning from the brocades and jewels that had been the staple materials for such spectacles in the past, Truscott used less opulent fabrics that were more suitable for the primitive court of King Arthur. Using roughly loomed woolens, raw silk, coarse linen, and crocheted lace, often trimmed with wild animal furs and leather and decorated with handmade barbaric jewelry, he achieved an eclectic effect, unexpected and exciting. For one scene he gave Miss Redgrave a full-cut winter cape of nubby white wool lavished with white goat fur, and her wedding dress was a gown made entirely of hand-crocheted natural-colored linen lace, decorated with minuscule seashells and pumpkin seeds. Truscott's ingeniously designed costumes brought him the 1967 Academy Award for best design in a color film.

One of the biggest trend-setting films of the sixties was Warner Brothers' 1967 production of love, murder, and country music, *Bonnie and Clyde*. With Warren Beatty, Faye Dunaway, Gene Hackman, Michael J. Pollard, and Estelle

The film version of Camelot *(1967) starred Richard Harris and Vanessa Redgrave in costumes by John Truscott. (Photo courtesy of Warner Bros. Inc. Copyright © 1967 by Warner Bros. Inc.)*

Parsons as a quintet of bank-robbing renegades of the early thirties, Theodora Van Runkle's nostalgic, somewhat "camp" costumes started a mild fashion revolution. Almost overnight, young ·people searched thrift shops, attic trunks, and Grandma's closets for remnants of twenties apparel, and soon off-beat boutiques sprang up everywhere with reproductions of the film's poor-people wardrobe for sale at highly inflated prices. Miss Van Runkle was nominated for an Academy Award for *Bonnie and Clyde*, and in 1974 was similarly honored for her designs for Paramount's *The Godfather, Part II*. That same year she created the witty costumes for the Warner Brothers' production of Jerry Herman's musicalization of Patrick Dennis's stage success *Auntie Mame*, with Lucille Ball bouncing about as its rambunctious heroine. A talented painter, Miss Van Runkle's sketches are more character studies than mere costume plates and are high-

Designer Theadora Van Runkle started a mild fashion revolution with her evocative, slightly camp early-thirties fashions for Bonnie and Clyde *(1967), which starred Faye Dunaway and Warren Beatty. (Photo courtesy of Warner Bros. Inc. Copyright © 1967 by Warner Bros. Inc.)*

ly prized by collectors. Among her other screen credits are *I Love You, Alice B. Toklas; The Thomas Crown Affair;* and *Bullitt* (all 1968).

Some of the most successful films of the seventies have owed much of their popularity to an ambience of nostalgia. *Bonnie and Clyde, Funny Lady* (excellently designed by the team of Ray Aghayan and Bob Mackie, 1975), *The Great Gatsby* (for which designer Theoni V. Aldredge won 1974's Academy Award), *The Way We Were* (Moss Mabry–Irene Sharaff, 1974), *The Sting* (Edith Head, 1973, an Academy Award winner), *Death in Venice* (Piero Tosi, 1971, an Academy Award nominee), *Chinatown* (Anthea Sylbert, 1974), and *Murder on the Orient Express* (Tony Walton, 1974) were all set in periods that look more romantic than today. Some, like *Bonnie and Clyde* and *The Great Gatsby*, were highly publicized for their wardrobes. Paramount spent many thousands of dol-

Robert Redford stars as the mysterious, restless Jay Gatsby in Paramount's 1974 film The Great Gatsby. *Ralph Lauren designed the perfectly tailored suits that were so important to Gatsby's image. (*The Great Gatsby *©*

lars touting Ms. Aldredge's costumes for *Gatsby*, with department-store exhibitions of the garments and magazine and newspaper feature articles extolling her recreation of F. Scott Fitzgerald's flamboyant world of the twenties. Certainly, proper credit in this instance must be given to Ralph Lauren also; he provided the men's costumes and, in the case of Robert Redford particularly, did an unparalleled job.

The world of Hollywood has undergone tremendous changes since the twenties and thirties. As the thirties ended, with a year of film making that included the monumental *Gone With the Wind*, the forties and World War II saw the inevitable decline of the great studio complexes—and the beginning of the end of the legendary Hollywood movie magic that had held the world in a happy trance.

150

Mia Farrow as Daisy Buchanan in The Great Gatsby *was elegantly costumed by Theoni Aldridge, who won the 1974 Academy Award for her evocation of the Jazz Age. She re-created the style of the twenties' flapper in every detail for Miss Farrow.* (The Great Gatsby © MCMLXXIV by Newdon Company. All rights reserved)

Many factors contributed to the decline and fall of the motion picture empire—as it *was*, that is, on the brink of the forties. The war siphoned off from the studios many talented people and the necessary materials needed for the sky's-the-limit, pull-out-all-the-stops kind of productions that had been the main artery of Hollywood's great solid-gold heart. Greatly increased union demands ate into the capital reserves of the major studios, forcing them in turn to lay off thousands of employees. More and more stringent budgets were set for films, and, in contrast to the past, there seemed to be no reprieve from these financial limitations. The resident chief costume designer disappeared from movie studios. Only Edith Head would (and still does) continue in this capacity at Universal. It is significant that during the seventies, every other costume designer who appeared on the list of Academy Award nominees was a free-lancer working on a single-picture contract. The same is also true of art directors, cinematographers, and special artisans.

It is estimated that in 1947, eighty-five million people went to the movies weekly. By 1960 that figure had shrunk to less than forty million. No longer hampered by the war effort, the manufacture of television sets was resumed in 1946 and expanded rapidly. The bland TV dinner replaced the mounds of fragrant buttered popcorn that had for generations been indispensable to watching Garbo and Gilbert, Crawford and Gable, Fred and Ginger, Myrna and William, Jeanette and Nelson, Judy and Mickey, and Monty and Liz. American families began to prefer to spend their Sunday nights with Ed Sullivan and Tuesday eve-

151

nings with Milton Berle to heading off for the local Bijou. It is not surprising that MGM's once-powerful and fearsome mogul Louis B. Mayer disappeared behind the stucco walls of his secluded Beverly Hills mansion, an aging and self-exiled emperor. Mayer, whose motto had been "Make it big, do it right, give it class," died in 1957, a mysterious recluse.

By the mid-seventies, some of Hollywood's major studios had become ghost towns. Only skeleton staffs consisting mostly of maintenance crews and security guards still wandered the once-thriving streets. Universal Studios continued to operate, but on a much more limited basis. Edith Head remains as chief designer at Universal, but her main activity now seems to be as a free-lance designer. Jack Warner sold his rights to Warner Brothers, reputedly for fifty-eight million dollars. Retiring to his Pasadena estate, Warner made an attempt in 1970 to invade Broadway when he produced an elaborate musical built on the life of New York's playboy mayor James Walker. Though Warner spent well over one million dollars of his personal fortune to bring *Jimmy* to the stage of Broadway's Winter Garden Theatre, it opened to poor reviews and closed after a few months.

By 1969, MGM was on the verge of bankruptcy. In the spring of that year it held its now famous auction of props and costumes. Collectors from across the country (and a number from Europe) descended on the MGM lot and eagerly bid for the stores of Adrians and creations of Helen Rose and Walter Plunkett. Soundstage 25 was transformed into an enormous sales area in which MGM's entire stock wardrobe was sold off at bargain prices. Much of the glamorous apparel could later be seen worn by hippies and UCLA students.

Unfortunately, over the years an equally inglorious fate befell many of the superb studio research libraries. These resources had been vital to producers, directors, writers, and technicians as well as to designers and craftsmen. Shelf after shelf had held bound volumes of American and European fashion publications, files of photographs, folios of original drawings of apparel, catalogues and illustrated trade pamphlets, and hundreds of books relating to historic periods and manner of dress. Carefully catalogued and supervised by professional librarians, these collections were impressive, yet by the mid-sixties most of them had either disappeared or been sold. In one case at least, hundreds of rare books were simply tossed out, left in waste containers at the street curb. A retired long-time studio librarian sadly remarked later: "At the time, nobody cared. The past was something to laugh at and forget. Of course, it's different now—but it's too late. You see, they sold or threw out their own history."

The ending of the great Hollywood movie studios marked, of course, the demise of the studio costume designer. Today, independently produced movies use the services of a great number of efficient if often uninspired wardrobe-oriented workers. Although the credits read "Costume Designer," "Wardrobe by . . ." or "Stylist," most clothes are simply bought from a department store or an arrangement is made whereby a well-known manufacturer will supply a male star's wardrobe for a line of credit among the screen titles of the film. The director and production manager generally select who will costume a film, and their decision is usually based almost solely on cost or whether the "designer" will be a compatible member of the small team that makes movies today. Only when a large-budget film with an important star is made is a well-known movie costumer called in: Edith Head, perhaps; Irene Sharaff, in rare instances; or the team of Aghayan and Mackie, who run their own workshops and are able to dress a movie quickly and for a fairly modest sum. And of course there is always the Western Costume Company in Los Angeles, or the Brooks-Van Horn or Eaves costume companies in New York, where thousands of period costumes made for past stage and screen productions are available for rental.

Some believe there is a definite resurgence of interest in the big, "old-fashioned" kind of movie that once poured out of Hollywood's famed studios. Certainly it is true that movie budgets have reached an all-time high and that often years are spent in making a film. But the budget is devoted mainly to the creation of immense mechanical white sharks, ocean liners that turn upside down in mid-ocean, earthquakes, exploding dirigibles, and all sorts of peculiar goings on in outer space. There is very little need for beautiful costumes in these kinds of thrillers, for it is to the Saturday-afternoon-serial kind of cliff-hanger that movie audiences look today. There are rare and beautiful exceptions, but they occur less and less frequently.

Yet there is a growing appreciation of the movies made during Hollywood's most productive and creative years. As art pieces they will never again be equaled, and such overwhelming response as to the Hollywood-costume exhibition held at New York's Metropolitan Museum of Art in 1975 ("Romantic and Glamorous Hollywood Design"), for which Diana Vreeland assembled a superb collection of opulent and thrilling golden-years' movie garments in an exhibition that broke all attendance records at that venerable institution, indicates that masses of people hunger to view the glorious artifacts of a splendor that only movies could once provide.

In January 1973, Paramount threw a party reminiscent of their more notable years to honor the one hundredth birthday of Adolph Zukor, their founding father and one of Hollywood's few remaining moguls. The event, produced by former head of studio Howard W. Koch, set Paramount's immense Melrose Avenue studios humming with activity once again. The evening's celebration included an elaborate dinner for fifteen hundred motion picture celebrities, a specially written mini-musical review, an eleven-foot-high birthday cake topped by one hundred candles, a documentary film with an assemblage of film clips from Zukor's most memorable productions, klieg lights, an endless cortege of limousines, and hundreds of fans waiting to gawk at and cheer the legion of movie stars who attended.

Seated on the rostrum of honored guests, the usually vivacious Edith Head, the only staff designer left at a major studio, looked a bit wistful when "Papa" Zukor was honored for the marvel he had helped bring to the world. Did she, perhaps, miss her peers who had made such a substantial contribution to film history? Associates like Adrian, Banton, Greer, Orry-Kelly, Irene, and Walter Plunkett?

Greta Garbo and John Gilbert in MGM's 1927 Love, *costumed by Adrian.*

Joan Crawford with Clark Gable in Possessed *(MGM, 1931).*

Myrna Loy and William Powell, a popular team in the Thin Man *series.*

Judy Garland and Mickey Rooney in MGM's 1940 Strike Up the Band.

Elizabeth Taylor and Montgomery Clift, cheek to cheek in A Place in the Sun *(Paramount, 1951).*

Jeanette MacDonald and Nelson Eddy in MGM's Maytime *(1937).*

Fred Astaire and Ginger Rogers, costumed by Plunkett in The Story of Vernon and Irene Castle *(RKO, 1939)*.

157

Diana Vreeland and Gloria Swanson admiring one of Adrian's designs at the Metropolitan Museum of Art's Hollywood costume exhibition of 1975. (Photograph by Ellen Graham)

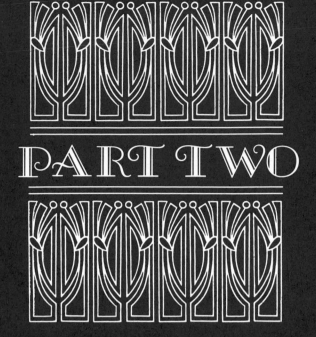

PART TWO

THE
DESIGNERS

A studio portrait of two of MGM's most valuable assets: Adrian, and his favorite responsibility, Greta Garbo. Taken in 1930, this publicity shot shows Adrian as a serious, dark-haired young man; Garbo, already a top star, in a rare instance reveals her slender, attractive legs.

1903-1959

ADRIAN

ADRIAN ADOLPH GREENBURG WAS BORN OF GERMAN-JEWISH PARENTS IN 1903 in Naugatuck, Connecticut. His father ran a thriving millinery shop and aspired to having his son graduate from Yale Law School. But at an early age Adrian demonstrated a natural ability to paint and draw, and by the time he was eighteen he had enrolled at the New York School of Fine and Applied Art (now the Parsons School of Design).

During his first summer vacation, Adrian accepted an opportunity to design costumes for the Gloucester Playhouse. There he had the satisfaction of seeing his designs realized for the first time, and he was encouraged by the group's manager, Florence Cunningham, who predicted he would have a future as a theatrical designer. It was at her suggestion that he became Gilbert Adrian (Gilbert was his father's first name).

In school, Adrian's work was not particularly distinguished, perhaps because he was restless and even bored with his art classes. At his instructor's suggestion, Adrian transferred to the school's Paris affiliate on the Place des Vosges. This wise move proved of lasting significance to the designer's development. Adrian basked in the twenties' creative ambience of Paris, where he felt right at home. He later boasted of having become a Parisian within twenty minutes.

One highlight of the fall season in Paris was the annual *bal masqué* at the Opera House. For weeks Adrian worked on his costume, a fanciful *Scheherazade* creation with overtones of the sleek art *moderne* popularized by Erté. His creation was so spectacular that it drew both applause and the attention of another guest, Irving Berlin. Berlin invited Adrian to design costumes for his coming production of the *Music Box Revue* in New York.

Adrian accepted Berlin's offer at once and sailed home after only four months abroad. His reception by Charles LeMaire, Berlin's regular costume designer, was far from encouraging, however. LeMaire found Adrian's designs to be generally impractical for the stage but agreed to include a few of them in the revue. LeMaire would come to regret his early rejection of Adrian's talent. When LeMaire later went to work in Hollywood, Adrian, who was already in a top design position there, refused to accept him socially.

The costumes that Adrian designed for the *Music Box Revue* led to a commission to do a revue for John Murray Anderson's Greenwich Village Follies. He also was asked to dress George White's famous beauties for *Scandals*. At the same time, Adrian received his first offer to do a Hollywood film.

Natacha Rambova, wife of the matinee idol Rudolph Valentino, had come to New York with her husband to discuss production of *The Hooded Falcon*. Written and produced by Rambova for her famed husband, the film required a costume designer of special abilities. When a portfolio of Adrian's exotic costume sketches found its way to her, Rambova invited the designer to their sumptuous hotel suite and, after a brief interview, invited him to join them in California. A few days later Adrian was heading West on the Twentieth Century Limited with the Valentinos and their entourage of servants, secretaries, publicity representatives, managers—and Rambova's golden-leashed monkey.

After settling into a small apartment on Highland Avenue in Hollywood, Adrian began work on *The Hooded Falcon*. The film's setting was a recreation of a Moorish palace, and Valentino, bearded for the first time, was to wear the kind of sweeping robes that had proved so effective in *The Sheik*. Unfortunately, some time later the budget of the film was slashed in half—to $500,000—and, only days after that, the film was completely canceled.

Adrian's first film credits came in 1925 for Paramount's *Cobra* and *The Eagle*, both starring Valentino. For the latter he costumed the star as a Russian cossack; Valentino's dashing uniforms brought sighs from the female audience and his tall astrakhan hats started a fashion trend. Adrian himself was so pleased with the outfits that when Valentino's estate was auctioned after his death in 1926, he bought one of the flaring cossack coats he had designed for the film.

Adrian designed costumes for thirty films—including *The Merry Widow* with Mae Murray, and Cecil B. De Mille's *King of Kings*—before MGM entrusted him with dressing Greta Garbo in *A Woman of Affairs* (1928). Fascinated by Garbo's mystical aloofness, Adrian intuitively understood the sublime challenge she presented. Though Garbo had been beautifully costumed by Andre-Ani and Max Ree for *The Temptress* and *The Torrent* (both 1926), it was Adrian who really perceived her wonderfully glacial beauty and mysterious allure that

Adrian's sophisticated evening dress for Joan Crawford in Letty Lynton *(MGM, 1932).*

seemed to invite unveiling. Adrian soon became one of the actress's true friends and she became his particular triumph. "At first, they hung bangles and glass beads on her," Adrian said. "I saw that she was like a tree with deep roots—deep in the earth. Never put an artificial jewel or imitation lace on Garbo. It would do something to Garbo and her performance."

Adrian joined MGM in 1929 as head designer and stayed there until his retirement in 1942. Although he often worked on as many as five movies simulta-

The Philadelphia Story: *Adrian's sketch and gown for Katharine Hepburn (MGM, 1940)*.

neously, he was noted for his meticulous attention to detail. Even the linings of his clothes were made of silk, and it was rumored that the extras at MGM were often better dressed than the stars at certain other studios.

Another actress who became indelibly identified with Adrian designs in the thirties was Joan Crawford. Her white-organdy ruffled evening dress in *Letty Lynton* (1932) caused a sensation, and was copied commercially by a number of dress manufacturers. So were the broad-shouldered Adrian suits that she later wore with such authority. Miss Crawford was also the first to acknowledge Adrian's contribution to her screen image and his influence on her as an actress. "If I'm copied," she has said, "it's because of my clothes, and Adrian does those. Adrian taught me so much about drama. Everything must be simple, simple, simple. He made me conscious of the importance of simplicity."

Adrian eloped with actress Janet Gaynor in 1939. They soon became one of Hollywood's most popular couples, especially noted for their splendid dinner parties and Sunday breakfasts. As good friends of the Basil Rathbones and of Irving Thalberg and his wife, Norma Shearer, they occupied a special niche in the film colony.

Even before World War II changed the motion picture industry, Adrian sensed that the golden days of cinema were fading. Yet some of his best work was done in the late thirties.

The Women, Idiot's Delight, and *The Wizard of Oz* appeared in 1939, and *Ziegfeld Girl, New Moon,* and *The Philadelphia Story* followed in 1940. Then, with *Two-Faced Woman* in 1941, Adrian's film career came to an end. In that movie, Louis B. Mayer's insistence that Garbo's screen image be brought down to earth, a badly written scenario, uninspired direction by George Cukor, and Mayer's constant, petulant interference all foreshadowed a future that neither Garbo nor Adrian cared to face. After a particularly horrendous conference with Mayer over the costumes for *Two-Faced Woman,* Adrian tore up the sketches on his drawing table and resigned. Garbo left the studio when the film was completed.

Mayer fumed, screamed with rage, threatened law suits, and finally wept at the loss of his top designer and illustrious star, but there was no turning back for either of them. "I got out," the designer stated later, "when I began to see the tin underneath the gold plate."

Fortunately, Adrian had been able to accumulate enough money to establish an impressive custom salon on Wilshire Boulevard. It was located in a white building with his distinctive signature scrawled across the side in bronze script. Although he had been cautioned about going into business so soon after America's entry into the war, Adrian profited handsomely by his decision, grossing more than two million dollars a year. He also manufactured expensive clothes that were retailed throughout the country.

Occasionally Adrian returned to films on a free-lance basis. In 1952 he costumed the principals and a fashion show sequence in *Lovely to Look At* for MGM. But shortly thereafter, Adrian gave up Hollywood altogether and retired with his wife to a plantation villa in Brazil, near the ranch of Mary Martin and her husband, Richard Halliday. There he was able to indulge in two of his favorite pastimes, interior design and gardening.

In 1959 he came out of retirement to design the costumes for Lerner and Loewe's Broadway musical *Camelot.* The Arthurian romance was a perfect vehicle for Adrian's talent in period costuming, but the strain may have been too much for him. Without warning, he suffered a heart seizure, was hospitalized, and died on September 13, 1959. By then, most of the costumes had been finished, a worthy testament to the designer's extraordinary talent.

Hollywood mourned Adrian's death—his work was symbolic of the best it could produce. The close friend who telephoned the sad news to Garbo recalled, later, the star's gasp, her attempt to speak, and then the click of the phone as it was placed back on the receiver.

One of the few Hollywood mementoes that Garbo is said to have kept is a pair of mauve kid gloves that she wore as Camille. Adrian sent them to her after the film was completed. Hand sewn and lined in silk, the gloves bear an inimitable Adrian touch: motifs of flowering vines worked in minuscule steel beads and seed pearls adorn each cuff, and upon close examination the delicate tendrils reveal the intertwined initials GG.

It is not surprising that when Garbo was given a private view of movie costumes on exhibit at the Metropolitan Museum, she was moved to lightly touch one of the dresses that Adrian had created for her. It was the cream-colored silk faille ball gown, bordered in sable, that she had worn as Camille.

Travis Banton confers with Marlene Dietrich in 1937. Banton considered Miss Dietrich the greatest inspiration any designer could hope for, and she reciprocated by consulting him about every detail of her wardrobe of both screen and personal clothes.

1894-1958

TRAVIS BANTON

AESTHETICALLY, TRAVIS BANTON HAD FEW RIVALS. HE PRODUCED CLOTHES of timeless beauty that were remarkable for their cut, exquisite fabric, and understated elegance. His garments were noted more for their subtle glow or shimmer than for dazzling sparkle or shine. Dresses that clung to the body in a soft bias cut were a particular Banton trademark. To highlight the intricate shapes of his designs, Banton usually chose fabrics of medium tones.

Born in Texas, Banton was taken to New York at the age of two, when his parents left Waco for Manhattan. Fortunately, his exposure to city life included regular trips with his mother to theater matinees—outings that left him stage-struck for life. Even when his career eventually led him to the movies, Banton always reminisced about seeing such performers as Julia Marlowe in *Cleopatra* and Hazel Dawn in *The Pink Lady*.

As a teenager, Banton began to paint and draw with facility, but he received little encouragement from his parents, who envisioned a business career for their son. When he was sixteen they enrolled him in a course of academic studies at Columbia University. However, it soon became obvious that he was unsuited for academic life, and he later admitted "hating every minute of it." He was allowed to transfer to the Art Students League, where he took classes in drawing and painting. There his proclivity for fashion design became apparent almost immediately. To the surprise of his drawing instructors, Banton embellished his female nude studies with flowing gowns, jewelry, and other fashion accessories!

At the urging of his teachers, Banton then began classes in fashion design, and from that moment on his life's focus was set. While still a student, the fledgling designer made his first contribution to the movies: After meeting movie actress Norma Talmadge at a party and showing her some sketches, he was commissioned to do one of her costumes for the 1917 film *Poppy*.

Subsequent recognition came with an apprenticeship to Mme Francis, a successful custom dressmaker with a clientele of New York society women and popular actresses. Banton's original designs were enthusiastically received, and when one of his sketches for a wedding gown was selected by Mary Pickford for her marriage to Douglas Fairbanks, his career was established.

During World War I, Banton served briefly in the Navy, and then returned to New York. He worked for a number of custom apparel houses, including that of Lucile, whose salon also served as a training ground for Howard Greer.

The next step in Banton's career was his own dressmaking salon in New York's East Fifties. One of his first clients, a showgirl, brought his designs to the attention of her producer, Florenz Ziegfeld, and soon Banton was creating a number of elaborate spectacle costumes for the famed Follies. One of the costumes was made almost entirely of black coq feathers, a decoration he favored and later used for Marlene Dietrich's famous outfit in *Shanghai Express* (Paramount, 1932).

Walter Wanger of Paramount was the first producer to sign Banton for an entire movie—*The Dressmaker from Paris,* starring Leatrice Joy, with a scenario about haute couture and high-living in Paris that ended with a parade of gowns in a fashion show. Paramount publicized Banton as a French designer, and his screen debut was successful enough for Adolph Zukor to offer him a contract at $150 a week as second to Howard Greer, the studio's head designer. Banton accepted, found himself a small apartment on Fairfax Avenue near the studio, and in 1925 began his long career in the movies.

In 1927, when Greer left Paramount to open his own custom salon, Banton was promoted to the number-one design position, with the responsibility of dressing the studio's most illustrious stars. Among them were Pola Negri, Evelyn Brent, Bebe Daniels, Clara Bow, Ruth Taylor, and Nancy Carroll, all of whom he clothed imaginatively and with great sophistication. From the beginning, Zukor was extremely pleased with Banton's costumes for Paramount's stars, and his esteem proved to be an invaluable asset to the designer's career with the studio.

It was Paramount's astonishing roster of beautiful stars in the thirties, however, that provided the inspiration for his most famous creations. Wearing Banton's enchantingly elegant clothes, on the screen Zukor's actresses epitomized wit, intelligence, and beauty. Claudette Colbert, Marlene Dietrich, Carole Lombard, Gail Patrick, Sylvia Sidney, and Mae West appeared in a dazzling array of Banton's creations, unsurpassed for allure and uncontrived splendor. Among his signatures were a lavish use of polka dots and men's clothes for women (most notably, Marlene Dietrich).

170

For Mae West's first films, including *Night After Night* (1932), Banton gave the "peach of the New York stage" the look of irresistible tongue-in-cheek glamor that established her screen image. Fortunately, West's success was immediate, and her films revived Paramount's sagging fortunes enough to save it from bankruptcy.

Every year Banton went off to Paris to shop for fabrics and accessories. At Hermès he ordered dozens of pairs of exquisite kid gloves and handbags, and at fabric houses he bought lamés, silk chiffons, velvets, silk crêpes, sheer wool crêpes, and tweeds of all kinds. For *Shanghai Express,* Dietrich's bags and gloves were made to order by Hermès. On one trip, a furor erupted when Schiaparelli discovered that Banton had bought her favorite supplier's entire stock of bugle beads and rare fish-scale paillettes. As a peace offering, Banton sent the designer enough trim to finish her line for the season.

Banton's designs were also in demand off the screen, and his clients included Marlene Dietrich, Claudette Colbert, Kay Francis, and Lilyan Tashman. For years, Francis and Tashman were among Hollywood's "Best Dressed" women, and Banton was often seen with one or the other at parties and premieres, though he did not usually find large Hollywood social gatherings to his liking.

But Dietrich possessed a great sense of showmanship and loved fancy-dress parties, frequently going to great lengths to steal the scene whenever possible, and nothing made Banton happier than to indulge her in these caprices. His designs for her were always incredible: Once she was Leda, complete with a swan's head, her torso covered with thousands of tiny feathers, each carefully painted by hand to create a subtle shaded effect. Another time, as a white rose, Dietrich's body was encased in a full-length leotard covered with green bugle beads. The floating leaf-shaped sleeves of the costume were made of green silk veined with beads, and the headdress was made of large white-satin rose petals with seed pearls and iridescent paillettes.

On his birthday and at Christmas, stacks of gifts were delivered to Banton from Paramount's stars, grateful for the superb clothes he created for them. One year Dietrich sent diamond-and-emerald cufflinks and shirt studs, Lilyan Tashman presented him with an inscribed gold cigarette case, Kay Francis gave him a champion dachshund, and Carole Lombard a Dufy painting. He enjoyed luxury, spent a fortune furnishing his beautiful house, and gave small dinner parties that were models of elegance and intimacy, generating a new vogue in Hollywood entertaining. "No more than six 'swells' at one time," he would say.

Unfortunately, Banton had begun to drink heavily by the mid-thirties. There were stories of his disappearing for days at a time and then turning up exhausted and ill. Certainly such behavior must have contributed heavily to his eventual rejection by most of Hollywood's major producers and his ultimate withdrawal from the movies. His friends, especially Carole Lombard, stuck by him and did what they could to keep him sober, but he was never really able to stop the illness that slowly accelerated.

In 1938, after fourteen years at Paramount, Banton joined forces with Howard Greer as a private couturier. A year later he was signed on as a designer at Twentieth Century-Fox to costume Alice Faye in her musicals *Lillian Russell*

Sketch and gown for Dietrich in The Devil Is a Woman *(Paramount, 1935).*

A design for Claudette Colbert in The Gilded Lily *(1935).*

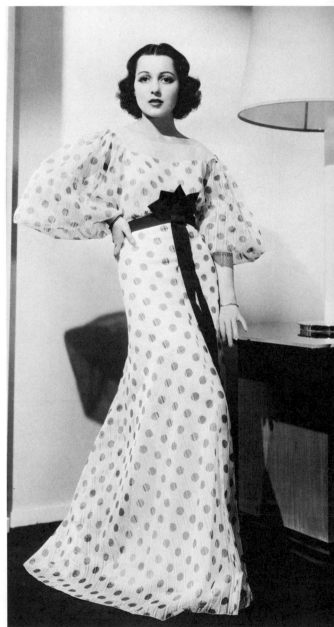

Among Banton's trademarks: polka dots (shown, left, on a 1936 gown worn by Frances Drake) and using men's clothes for women (especially Dietrich).

Banton's designs for Mae West brought instant success to both Paramount and its perennial star.

The drawing room of Travis Banton's Hollywood home reflected his personality and preferences for rare antiques, exquisite lamps, and paintings.

(1940) and *That Night in Rio* (1941). But the combination was not a happy one as Banton and Miss Faye clashed frequently; she insisted on clothes with flashy decoration, while he resisted what he considered vulgarization.

During one fitting Faye suggested wider bands of bugle-beaded arabesques on her gown, arguing that Dietrich's costumes were often glittery. Losing his patience, Banton coldly informed Faye that Dietrich could carry off any amount of decoration with her innate chic, but that such clothes on Faye would make her look like a "carnival hootch"! The enraged star took up the matter with Zanuck himself, who telephoned Banton and instructed him to give the often-petulant Faye more respectful treatment.

The 1890s diamanté-embellished gowns that Banton finally designed for Faye looked superb on her curvaceous figure, and she sent him a note of thanks with the hope that the two of them might work more compatibly. But the designer's

177

Merle Oberon insisted that Travis Banton dress her in her role of George Sand in Columbia's 1945 A Song to Remember. *Miss Oberon said of Banton: "He knew what the character ought to look like but also understood what an actress was happiest wearing, which is very rare for a costume designer. I never found it necessary to make a single change on one of his drawings."*

pride had been wounded by Zanuck's reprimand and he never forgave her. At Paramount, Adolph Zukor had backed him in any questions concerning changes on a costume, and, as Edith Head said, "nobody dared oppose Banton about anything." Banton's less exalted position at Fox was one he couldn't cope with. As a result, he left in 1941 to return to his private clientele. He continued to occasionally design for films, when one of his faithful stars demanded him for a picture. Carole Lombard, for one, insisted that he do her costumes at Universal and Warner Brothers, as well as for *Nothing Sacred* and *Made for Each Other,* produced by David Selznick.

From 1945 to 1948 (when he retired permanently from the movies) Banton was listed as a stylist at Universal, but such work was essentially carried out on a free-lance basis, in addition to his private business.

Banton returned home to New York in the early 1950s, where he designed sporadically but successfully, for a number of Seventh Avenue dress manufacturers. Had he so chosen, he might have begun a second career in that market, but he remained in semiretirement until 1956, when he returned to Hollywood and opened a custom salon with the stage designer Marusia. Together they costumed Rosalind Russell for her stage appearance in *Auntie Mame.* A year later Banton died of complications stemming from alcoholism.

During his later years, Banton confided to friends that he had perhaps tried to hang on too long, and that he would have been wiser to give up designing for movies about the same time Adrian did (in 1942). However, he admitted that, accustomed as he was to the expensive pleasures of Hollywood life, he could not have afforded to give up the generous salary he received designing for that medium.

During his long up-and-down career in Hollywood, Banton designed costumes for more than 160 movies. Those that follow are among the most memorable.

For Dietrich there were *Morocco* (1930), *Shanghai Express* (1932), *The Scarlet Empress* (1934), *Desire* (1936), and *Angel* (1937); for Claudette Colbert, *Cleopatra* (1934) and *The Gilded Lily* (1934). Also, he designed for Miriam Hopkins in *Design for Living* (1933); Carole Lombard in *No Man of Her Own* (1932), *Bolero* (1934), and *My Man Godfrey* (1936); and Mae West in *I'm No Angel* (1933) and *Belle of the Nineties* (1934).

Though he preferred designing movies with contemporary settings, Banton's period costumes—such as those for *So Red the Rose* (1935), *Lillian Russell* (1940), and *Letter from an Unknown Woman* (1948)—were often exceptional. But regardless of the subject, the combination of Banton's insistence on perfect workmanship and his own imaginative designs resulted in clothes that equaled the finest anywhere. Provocative yet elegant, his costumes remain among the most splendid ever seen on the screen.

A recent comment of Dietrich's is a fitting tribute. When asked to lend her white tail coat and top hat to an exhibition of Hollywood clothes at the Metropolitan Museum in New York, she declined, saying, "I still wear them in my act."

Cecil Beaton, 1973.

Beaton.

1904-1980

CECIL BEATON

Sir Cecil Beaton was a designer of costumes and scenery, a photographer, interior designer, illustrator, author, playwright, dilettante actor, and arbiter of all things fashionable.

The eldest of four children, Beaton was born on January 14, 1904, in the London suburb of Hampstead Heath, where he grew up enjoying the solid comforts provided by an upper-middle-class English family. It was a splendid time to be English: life was filled with pomp and good living, tempered daring, and change. Indelibly, it would remain in his memory throughout his life.

When Beaton was four, his father, who had been a notable amateur actor, took him to see the legendary Lily Elsie in a matinee performance of *The Merry Widow.* Upon watching Miss Elsie waltz in her Lucile gown of parfait-shaded chiffon sparkling with bugle beads, Beaton became permanently enamored of the theater.

At the age of ten he constructed a toy theater from a hatbox he discovered while visiting aunts in Worcestershire. He cut photographs of chorus ladies from *The Play Pictorial,* water-colored their faces for makeup, highlighted their costumes with gold and silver paint, and painted miniature rose-and-wisteria-covered scenery in imitation of the day's musical comedy rage, *Oh, Oh, Delphine.* "The characters were pushed on stage by means of tin clips attached to long handles," he later recalled. "It remained only to make them perform, which I did by acting all the parts and singing the score myself. Here in remote Arley, my theatrical dreams flourished. . . ."

By the time his schooldays at Harrow and the three years of half-hearted studies he spent at Cambridge University had ended, Beaton had already begun his involvement with the theater as a designer and actor. For a 1922 production of Thackeray's *The Rose and the Ring,* given by a dramatic society at Cambridge, he played the role of Princess Angelica *"en travesti"* and, according to a review in *The Daily Telegraph,* "did very well indeed." The following year he designed a production of *Volpone* for the University's Marlowe Society and this time *The Daily Telegraph* declared his efforts "worthy of a London stage." He continued to act in amateur productions and design costumes and décor for a number of them while pursuing a highly successful career as a portrait and fashion photographer.

At age thirty Beaton made his professional debut as a theatrical designer, with several scenes in the famed London producer C. B. Cochran's 1934 revue, *Streamline.* This was followed by other assignments from Cochran, ballets for Osbert Sitwell and William Walton, and a collaboration in 1936 with the choreographer Frederick Ashton for his ballet *Apparitions* at the Sadler's Wells Theatre in London. That same year he designed the sets and costumes for a ballet Ashton choreographed for Cochran's *Follow the Sun,* and for a production of the Kochno-Lichine ballet *Le Pavillon* for Basil's Ballets Russes de Monte Carlo. Also in 1936 Beaton successfully held his first exhibition of theater designs, at the Redfern Gallery in London.

During World War II, Beaton's activities as an official military photographer assigned to various parts of the theaters of war did not prevent him from also continuing his work for London's West End theaters. In 1941, Gabriel Pascal commissioned him to design the costumes for his film version of George Bernard Shaw's *Major Barbara* (with Wendy Hiller, Deborah Kerr, and Rex Harrison). That same year Beaton also costumed the films *Kipps,* directed by Carol Reed and starring Diana Wynyard and Michael Redgrave, and *Dangerous Moonlight,* directed by Brian Desmond Hurst, with Sally Gray and Anton Walbrook. In 1942, Carol Reed used Beaton as costumer again, for the movie *The Young Mr. Pitt,* with Robert Donat and Robert Morley. When Clive Brook both directed and starred in *On Approval* in 1944, with a cast that also included Beatrice Lillie, Googie Withers, and Roland Culver, Beaton was responsible for their delightful turn-of-the-century costumes.

After the war, in 1946, Beaton was designer of both sets and costumes for an American stage production of Oscar Wilde's *Lady Windermere's Fan,* and Somerset Maugham's *Our Betters* in London. Beaton also designed the costumes for Maurice Elvey's film *Beware of Pity,* starring Lilli Palmer. In 1948 he was costume designer for the movie of Wilde's *An Ideal Husband,* directed by Alexander Korda with Paulette Goddard, Michael Wilding, and Glynis Johns; and Julien Duvivier's screen version of Tolstoy's *Anna Karenina,* starring Vivien Leigh in the role played on the screen earlier by Greta Garbo.

Beaton would not design for the screen again until 1958, when Vincente Minnelli asked him to act as both set and costume designer for *Gigi,* starring Leslie Caron as Colette's young heroine. For more than two months Beaton worked at his beautiful English country estate, Reddish House, sketching the costume designs for the film. A thorough researcher, he drew on early periodicals—*Les Modes, Femina, Le Théâtre,* and *Cahiers d'Art*—to inspire his highly original interpretations of the period's fashions. Sketches for the film's principal roles were sent to the Paris atelier of Mme Karinska, Beaton's favorite costumer, and he often went there himself to observe her progress. Later he settled in at MGM to oversee the execution of many other designs for the film.

At the Hollywood studio, Beaton delightedly explored the vast wardrobe-storage rooms for accessories, props, and an occasional costume. One of his discoveries was a severe black gown that was perfect for Hermione Gingold as Gigi's aunt. Highly sensitive, Miss Gingold complained that the simple black wool dress was shabby, worn, and devoid of elegance, "Almost like a school mistress' uniform." She was right, of course, but, as Beaton knew, the costume was ideally suited to the character, and it lent an air of Gallic thrift to her. It also made her stand out strongly against the film's colorful décor, a nuance that Miss Gingold might not have anticipated. At any rate, Minnelli supported Beaton, while Hermione fumed on.

Beaton won the Academy Award for best costume design in *Gigi,* establishing a permanent place for himself among Hollywood's great designers. He returned to Hollywood to design *My Fair Lady* (1964) for Warner Brothers with astounding success. For his efforts Beaton received two Academy Awards: one for his costumes and another for his brilliant job as the film's art director.

Very seldom have a film's costumes stirred the critics and audiences to such expressions of praise as did those Beaton created for *My Fair Lady*. His designs for Audrey Hepburn, romantic and provocative evocations of the fashions of the Edwardian world he knew and loved so well, must certainly rank among the most successful ever captured on film. The famed Ascot black-and-white ensemble brought gasps from moviegoers everywhere, and Eliza's white silk ribbon-lace gown and immense hat trimmed with poppies and clusters of lilacs has become a classic.

Sadly, Beaton was not to design what might have been his most extraordinary assignment. In 1948, Greta Garbo seriously considered returning to the screen in a film based on the life of Austria's tragic Empress Elizabeth. With Alexander Korda producing, Beaton had been selected to design the project's sets and to costume his close friend for her role. Together, actress and designer looked at engravings and drawings of the empress, Garbo making frequent observations about her clothes ("Look at the line of the *naickke,* how straight she holds her head back on her shoulders. You see she wears the necklace short; I don't like them when they hang loose on the chest. . . . " "What is lovely is that wide crown—how chic").

But the hoped-for collaboration ultimately was not possible because of a prior commitment made by Korda. Instead, Garbo was offered the role of Madame

Sketch by Beaton for Audrey Hepburn's portrayal of Eliza selling flowers at Covent Garden, before her transformation at the hands of Henry Higgins, and photograph by Beaton of Hepburn in costume.

The famous Ascot dress, as sketched and photographed by Beaton.

Ranevska in a filming of Chekhov's *The Cherry Orchard*. Garbo and Beaton read the play together and discussed how she might be costumed, aspects of the décor, her hair styles. Then, inexplicably, Garbo rejected the role. She had no enthusiasm for the play, and that would be that.

It was a bitter disappointment for Beaton and a great loss to the millions who had hoped to once again see Garbo's special incandescence fill a movie screen. With Garbo costumed by Beaton and playing against his sets, a film combining the talents of two such unique artists could only have been a treasure.

Beaton again returned to Hollywood to design the costumes and sets for the period sequences in the film version of Alan Jay Lerner's Broadway musical *On a Clear Day You Can See Forever* (1970). Produced at Paramount by Howard W. Koch, with Vincente Minnelli directing and Barbra Streisand as its star, Beaton's contribution to the film proved to be its most successful element. Shot in England amid the fantastic Chinese splendors of the Royal Pavilion at Brighton, Beaton's Regency costumes for Streisand brought her a new and impressive elegance on the screen. A ball gown of white silk embroidered with silver beads and pearls perfectly epitomizes the kind of magic Beaton can create and is one of the most beautiful costumes ever designed for a movie.

A year earlier, Beaton had similarly brought an undiscovered chic to the legendary Katharine Hepburn when he costumed her for Alan Jay Lerner's 1969 Broadway production *Coco,* a musical biography of the French couturière Chanel. Hepburn was known to dislike "dressing up" for her roles, and Beaton faced the formidable task of transforming her into one of the most famed designers of the century. It was a difficult and sometimes tense challenge, but he succeeded admirably—and received a Tony award for his characteristically elegant job. Kate never looked better!

In 1973, Cecil Beaton was honored by Queen Elizabeth II with knighthood. It was a gratifying reward for his many years of creative successes and one that was richly deserved. Sadly, his life took a downturn that year, when he suffered a stroke. Though paralyzed on the right side, Sir Cecil refused to accept invalidism and persisted in writing and editing his diaries for publication. At his spacious and famed estate near Salisbury in Wiltshire, he mastered writing and painting with his left hand, with astonishing dexterity.

In 1976 a full and superbly produced Broadway revival of *My Fair Lady,* under the auspices of its original producer, Herman Levin, once again brought Beaton's original costumes before cheering audiences.

A total artist, Sir Cecil Beaton made a distinguished and lasting contribution to both theater and motion pictures as a designer. His creative genius has fortunately been captured forever on film, to delight and astonish future audiences.

Barbra Streisand, superbly costumed by Cecil Beaton for the Regency ball scene in Paramount's 1970 On a Clear Day You Can See Forever. *(Photograph by Cecil Beaton)*

Howard Greer. (Photograph by Tom Kelley)

HOWARD GREER

HOWARD GREER ARRIVED IN HOLLYWOOD LATE IN 1923 TO DESIGN THE COStumes for Pola Negri's first American film, *The Spanish Dancer.* Knowledgeable in the ways of designing for fashionable, demanding women, the thirty-seven-year-old New York defector looked upon the venture as a new, amusing kind of challenge. And he met it famously.

Greer's fashion career began when he was quite young. He had already developed his own style of drawing and decided to write for an interview with Lucile, the eccentric English dressmaker who had salons in Chicago, New York, London, and Paris. Lucile, whose marriage to a wealthy member of the English peerage had graced her with the title of Lady Duff-Gordon, answered affirmatively by telegram under her cable name Lucilation. Greer cabled back: DEATH ALONE WILL KEEP ME FROM YOU THURSDAY, and a week later he left Lincoln, Nebraska, for Lucile's plush salon on Lake Shore Drive in Chicago.

Although nervous at the prospect of meeting the imperious Lucile, Greer nonetheless managed to make a favorable impression with his fashion drawings and became a sketcher-apprentice in the Chicago salon. In 1918 he was transferred to the New York workrooms on Fifth Avenue at Twenty-Second Street, where he felt truly free to design in earnest. The first day in New York Greer wept with joy.

His happiness came to an abrupt end a year later, however, when he was drafted into the army and sent to France, where he fought in the horrendous battle of Château-Thierry. When World War I ended, the designer remained in France, working in Lucile's new salon on the Rue de Penthièvre in Paris. He found a properly chilly studio with a skylight on the Rue Boissonade, not far from the center of activity on the Left Bank, and settled into the famous Paris of the twenties. Among the new tastes he acquired was a liking for wine and absinthe, a fondness that became excessive later in his life.

Lucile's salon soon became a gathering place for the demimonde, who found her assistant amusing, with his casual Midwestern manners. Lucile herself had decorated the new quarters; the walls, curtains, and furniture were done in a Swiss gray that was enhanced by a thick purple carpet. It was an environment that suited the socialites, actresses, courtesans, drawing-room Marxists, Oriental mystics, Greek purists, hangers-on, clawers-up, and second-class royalists who frequented the place. As for Greer, he confessed, "It was the day of Picasso and Picabia, and I was carried away by anything I didn't understand."

Greer also got around. Paul Poiret, the czar of French fashion, invited him to a soirée and gave him a signed photograph. Queen Marie of Romania poured tea for him in the garden of Elsie de Wolf's house at Versailles, and Yvonne Printemps invited the designer to visit a Left Bank dive to hear the sensational new *jazz hot* with her. He was also a regular at the Sunday afternoon gatherings in the lavish Quai Voltaire apartment of Cécile Sorel, a leading actress of the Comédie Française, where he mingled with such luminaries as Jean Cocteau, Isadora Duncan, Gaby Deslys, and Maurice Ravel.

Then an unfortunate incident provoked the dissolution of Greer's association with Lucile. Called away from Paris on business, Lucile entrusted the care of her ancient Pekinese dog to Greer. Shortly after she left, Greer was confined to bed with pneumonia, and when Lucile returned, the pet had expired. In a rage she accused Greer of neglect and dismissed him with a warning that she would denounce him publicly if he ever approached her again. After several years she relented, and the two renewed their friendship, but Greer never worked with her again.

In need of a warmer climate, Greer found his way to Monte Carlo, where he managed to find a job painting in the painstaking details of Erté's illustrations for the covers of Hearst's fashion magazine, *Harper's Bazaar*. Displeased with Greer's work, Erté refused to pay him, but let him have a discarded illustration instead. On second thought Erté demanded his drawing back and gave Greer a five-hundred-franc note.

Sometime later, while wandering past the shops on the Croisette, Greer discovered the Monte Carlo boutique of Paul Poiret. He presented himself and his sketches to Poiret, who amazed Greer by paying him six hundred francs for the lot and extending an invitation to a *fête d'or* at the casino the following night. Greer accepted, and lost every sou playing roulette.

His windfall gone, Greer returned to Paris to try his hand at writing interviews with theater personalities for an American magazine. Friends Cécile Sorel and Yvonne Printemps let him write pieces about them, and Sorel arranged for Greer to see Sarah Bernhardt. But this new venture did not prove lucrative enough for Greer to survive comfortably, so, broke and a bit homesick, he made plans to sail back to America.

On his return to New York, the designer rented a small basement apartment on Waverly Place in Greenwich Village and managed to subsist by creating custom apparel for wealthy women, including many he had met abroad. Greer also investigated the possibility of designing costumes for stage revues, an idea that had intrigued him ever since he had seen the costumes Lucile devised for the Ziegfeld Follies.

Learning that John Murray Anderson planned to produce a cabaret revue, Greer sketched a number of costumes, showed them to Anderson—and was hired as a designer for twenty-five dollars a week. Anderson was so pleased with Greer's work that he retained the designer for his next venture, *The Greenwich Village Follies of 1922;* Greer was also assigned to create some of the scenery. With music written by the new songwriting team of Rodgers and Hart and conducted by another fledgling, Alfred Newman, the production was a resounding success.

Greer's theatrical coup and his past associations with Molyneux, Poiret, and Lucile brought increasing numbers of clients to his modest dressmaking studio. Suddenly he found himself vying with Gilbert Clarke, an Englishman who was one of New York's most popular small-scale custom designers. Clarke, in turn, was alarmed by the number of clients deserting him for the more original clothes of his competitor. So, when Clarke was offered the chance to dispose of his business and move to California to design for the Famous Players movie company, he cannily suggested that Greer might be a better candidate. At the time, movies were still considered an unfashionable medium, and Clarke's recommendation was not intended as a compliment. Later, however, when Greer became famous as Paramount's designer, Clarke claimed credit for his discovery.

Walter Wanger, the young assistant to Jesse Lasky, who was president of Famous Players, interviewed Greer and signed him on for a trial period of six weeks at the rate of two hundred dollars a week. Greer then hired Edith Head as his assistant for fifty dollars weekly. Greer later wrote, "Well, six weeks wasn't a lifetime and at the end of it I could come back to New York, with a sizable bankroll." As it turned out, he stayed on for years.

Greer's first assignment was to costume Pola Negri in *The Spanish Dancer.* The fiery "La Negri" had refused to be dressed by a regular wardrobe woman and had insisted on having an exclusive designer. To make her point, she had swept into the front office, screamed with rage, torn apart her pearls, and tottered on the verge of fainting. Greer had been hired to appease her, which he did with spectacular clothes. She was particularly happy with his pearl-and-crystal-embroidered brocade and lamé wedding dress with its ermine trim, fifteen-foot-long train, and towering mantilla of Val lace. According to studio publicity, the gown cost twenty-five thousand dollars and was apparently worth every penny.

A Greer costume sketch done in the twenties.

Lasky showed his gratitude by rewarding Greer with a raise and extending his trial contract. Designing for Negri would remain one of his favorite assignments.

For Hollywood's first important dramatic Western, *The Covered Wagon,* Greer was called on to create stark pioneer clothes. Many years later, the film's star, Lois Wilson, recalled the great care he had taken to see that her woolen skirt and knitted shawl were authentic. But, to protect her from its rough texture, he had the skirt lined in matching silk. "He was a perfectionist," she recalled. "Nothing escaped his attention, and his concern that a costume please the performer who had to wear it was a new thing in Hollywood at that time."

In 1924, Greer worked with Claire West on the costumes for De Mille's *The Ten Commandments.* By then Famous Players had become Paramount Pictures, and when West left the studio later that year to design for First National, Greer became chief designer.

Until his departure from Paramount in 1927, Greer designed for a roster of stars that included Billie Dove, Leatrice Joy, Louise Brooks, Clara Bow, and

Pola Negri in Greer's famed wedding gown for The Cheat *(Paramount, 1923).*

Bebe Daniels. With his training in fine dressmaking from Lucile, he was the first movie designer to organize and staff a studio wardrobe unit that maintained high professional standards. It was such high caliber design departments that nurtured the talents of designers like Adrian, Banton, Head, and Orry-Kelly, who produced the great film costumes of the golden thirties and the forties.

One of Greer's closest associates was Travis Banton, who had been brought from New York to costume *The Dressmaker from Paris* (1925). As co-workers at Paramount, Banton and Greer got along famously, perhaps because their lives had so many parallels. Both men had come to New York from small towns west of the Mississippi and had apprenticed with successful custom dressmakers. Both had served in World War I, attempted to establish an independent design studio, designed showgirl costumes for the Follies and been brought to Hollywood by Walter Wanger on a one-picture trial contract at Paramount.

Both men also loved elegance and fine living, and shared a disdain for Hollywood's often gauche high society. Each was happiest in New York or Paris shopping extravagantly, viewing the collections, and indulging in fine restaurants, the theater, opera, and ballet. Greer frankly admitted to being a New York snob, and in later years Banton confessed privately that in Los Angeles he had "*loathed* those endless barbecue things, deadly-dull afternoons spent staring at people wallowing in swimming pools" and found the West Coast a place where "even the French champagne went flat as soon as it was poured."

In his book *Designing Male*, Greer wrote: "If I live another hundred years I doubt whether I will develop a 'camera-eye' and know, from its inception, whether an idea will live up to my expectations on celluloid. This wavering doubt over my brain children grew into a real obsession, and I began to think that Mr. Lasky's ax might fall across my neck at the very next option." To assuage his fears, Greer turned more and more to the bottle. Lasky, who was aware of Greer's drinking problem, summoned the designer to his office more than once for a heart-to-heart chat, and word quickly got around that Greer was on the way out.

The handwriting on the wardrobe wall was clear, and when Greer did not reform, a last warning, couched in the form of an interoffice memorandum, was handed to him by Wanger himself. To escape Lasky's now-poised ax, Greer announced he would not sign an extension of his contract. He also let it be known that he planned to open a custom dressmaking salon, though it had not occurred to him that he would have difficulty raising the funds necessary to organize a business. In retrospect, Greer sighed, "If I'd suspected all the agony and grief ahead of me . . . well, now that I think of it, I'd probably have done it anyway!"

To raise money for his salon, Greer designed the costumes for a revue at the Hollywood Music Box Theater. Fanny Brice was its star, and the soon-to-be-discovered Nancy Carroll and Lupe Velez were in the chorus line. Greer also did some custom designing, and eventually accumulated enough money to rent space for his salon in a new building on Sunset Boulevard. While it was being decorated in the same Swiss gray Lucile had chosen for her Paris showrooms,

Greer went to Europe. He bought perfumes to sell under his own label and also returned with dozens of bolts of expensive fabric. He hired four fitters, two tailors, fifty seamstresses, and five assistants to fashion the fabric into two hundred dresses for his first collection—three times the number of gowns shown at most French couture houses. It was a hectic but joyous time for Greer, who labored with new-found devotion to his own world of couture.

Finally, with all the hoopla and fanfare of a movie premiere, the opening took place on December 27, 1927. Klieg lights pierced the sky and a red-carpeted sidewalk led to the door. Hollywood's fearsome oracle Louella Parsons headed the by-invitation-only guest list of the town's upper crust, which included Norma Talmadge, Bessie Love, Lilyan Tashman, the Adolph Zukors, Vilma Banky, Prince and Princess Serge Mdivani, and Mae Murray. Tom Mix, wearing a purple dinner jacket over white pants and white tooled-leather cowboy boots, escorted his wife, whose costume included an immense corsage of poinsettias.

Five statuesque mannequins, with the provacative names of Mélisande, Babette, Corisande, Cécile, and Iaia, stepped off a chiffon-curtained stage to make their way through rooms filled with applauding celebrities. Greer named each of his creations in humorous fashion, such as "Whoops, Get Her!" 'and "Blind Nuns Under Water," and ended the show with a bridal gown, one of his specialities. (He later designed wedding dresses for Gloria Vanderbilt and Shirley Temple.) When the ovation at last subsided, Madge Bellamy rushed to buy thirty-one models, Bessie Love ordered seven chiffon evening gowns, and Ann Hardin bought three, in addition to two pairs of bugle-beaded crêpe smoking pajamas. When the last guest had left, the designer and his staff toasted the successful launching of Greer, Inc., with magnums of champagne.

In 1929, Mary Pickford turned from the "poor little waif" roles that had made her fortune, to play a Southern belle in United Artists' *Coquette,* her talkie debut. America's sweetheart was dressed by Greer to play an irresistible but vixenish heroine, and, according to Hedda Hopper, "knocked a lot of smart eggs flat on their behinds." After receiving an Academy Award for her performance, Pickford graciously acknowledged that Greer's costumes had helped bridge the perilous gap between her ingenue image and that of a mature dramatic actress.

Greer's next film assignment came from Hughes-United Artists to do *Hell's Angels* (1930). The movie was produced at the then considerable cost of more than a million dollars. Hughes first began it as a silent film in 1927, with Greta Nissen playing the lead (also in Greer's costumes), but he later replaced Nissen with an unknown platinum-haired nineteen-year-old girl named Harleen Carpenter from Kansas City, Missouri. Rechristened Jean Harlow, the girl soon became one of Hollywood's sensational beauties and another of Greer's private clients. When he made her a low-cut red velvet evening gown and a matching fox-trimmed wrap for the premiere of *Private Lives,* a newspaper writer covering the event rapturously described her as "a slender sphere of pure crystal wrapped in red garments borrowed for the evening from some clothes-closet in

Paramount player Greta Nissen in one of Greer's designs.

Hades." Greer promptly dubbed the remaining fabric in his storeroom "Mephisto Flame."

During the next five years, Greer contributed costumes to a number of films, including *The Animal Kingdom* (RKO, 1932, with Irene), *The Rich Are Always with Us* (Warner Brothers, 1932, with Orry-Kelly), *Page Miss Glory* (Warner Brothers, 1935, with Orry-Kelly, *Ann Vickers, Christopher Strong, The Silver Cord,* and *This Man Is Mine* (all in collaboration with Walter Plunkett at RKO, 1933 and 1934), and *Thirty Day Princess* (Paramount, 1934).

Meanwhile, Greer's salon demanded most of his time, and the guest book he had started as a gag continued to be filled with the names of the rich and famous. To Greer's astonishment, the elusive Garbo also appeared at his salon, with her friend Lilyan Tashman. She bought eighteen ensembles for a trip to Europe and was personally fitted by Greer, whose air of polite indifference to her star status favorably impressed her. She later accepted several invitations to dine at the designer's home.

Greer was the first important film designer to open a salon, and "Go to Greer" became standard advice for those aspiring to the ranks of the fashionable. Like his mentor, the savvy Lucile, Greer recognized the commercial value of snob appeal and let it be known that his clothes were expensive, required frequent fittings, and took four to six weeks to make. Invitations to the first showing of a new collection were sent only to valued customers, and the receipt of one could boost a climber several notches up movie town's slippery social ladder.

Exhausted by the demands of his salon and film work, Greer took two years off, from 1935 to 1937, to live in Paris, leaving his salon in the hands of an assistant. When he arrived in Paris, Greer called Banton in Hollywood to complain that "everything is still here except the people who made it fun."

When Greer returned to Hollywood he resumed both his custom designing and his film work. He dressed Katharine Hepburn in *Bringing Up Baby* (RKO, 1938) and co-designed *Holiday* (1938) with Kalloch for Columbia. He also did *Carefree* (1938) there, and then transferred to MGM for *Merrily We Live* (1938) which he co-designed with Irene.

When Travis Banton's tenure as Paramount's executive designer ended in 1938, Greer invited him to join his salon. "Howard didn't really need him at all," Hedda Hopper has said, "but he knew Travis was awfully depressed and worried about him. Howard's manager told me he had been afraid at the time they might start tooting it up with too many cocktails and the shop would suffer, but Travis started getting offers to do some pictures again and things worked out."

From 1939 to 1941, Greer worked for Universal, where he costumed *When Tomorrow Comes* and *Unfinished Business*. When the war depleted his staff of experts, he devoted himself full time to the salon. For Greer, who had fought in World War I, World War II was deeply disturbing. He bought bonds, worked at the Hollywood Canteen, made and contributed costumes for benefits and bond drives, but inevitably found escape in drink as well.

Greer returned to Universal to co-design 1944's *Follow the Boys* and *Christmas Holiday* with Vera West, and for Paramount he worked with Mary Kay Dodson on *Practically Yours.* The next year Alfred Hitchcock commissioned Greer to costume *Spellbound,* his highly successful venture into psychodrama (starring Ingrid Bergman and Gregory Peck).

Greer's next fashion venture was the idea of Bruce MacIntosh, a young New York sketch artist hired by the designer in 1946. MacIntosh wanted Greer to design a wholesale line. He agreed, reluctantly, and by 1947 he was making clothes for fifty-two exclusive franchise outlets in major cities throughout the country. Surprisingly, the venture turned out to be "more solacing, exciting, and profitable than . . . pictured." The profits were immense, far greater than those from his designs for movies and private customers. But when increasing maintenance costs and a shortage of skilled labor became too much to cope with, Greer, Inc., closed its doors.

The last three films Greer worked on, for RKO, were *Holiday Affair* (1949), *His Kind of Woman,* and *The French Line* (1951 and 1954, with Michael Woulfe as codesigner). Finally, in the mid-fifties, Greer retired. At home, close friends sought him out to reminisce about the Hollywood they had shared, but soon they, too, were gone: Travis Banton died in 1958, followed by Adrian in 1959, and Irene in 1962. All were members of what Greer referred to as "my clan," and on April 17, 1964, he joined them.

An evaluation of Greer's work was perhaps best expressed by the designer himself in his autobiography:

> New York and Paris disdainfully looked down their august noses at the dresses we designed in Hollywood. Well, maybe they *were* vulgar, but they *did* have imagination. If they were gaudy, they but reflected the absence of subtlety which characterized all early motion pictures. . . . No halfway measures here!. . . Into this carnivalesque atmosphere I was plummeted. There I wallowed in rhinestones and feathers and furs and loved every minute of it. . . . Every dress you make can't be a good one. After all, designing clothes is like baking cakes or painting pictures or writing songs: there are ups and downs to all trades and you can't always·have the critics with you. . . . For every luscious bloom there's been a fat, sharp thorn.

Near the end of his long career, Greer designed this beautiful Orient-inspired coat of embroidered silk over full trousers for Jane Russell (His Kind of Woman, RKO, 1951).

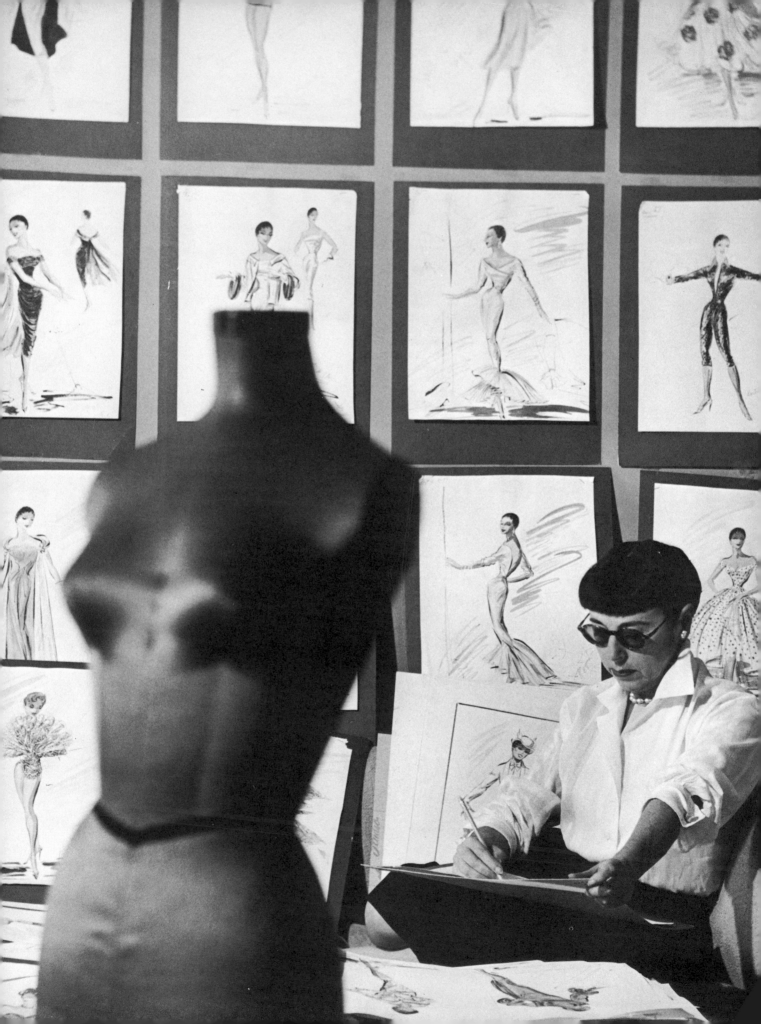

EDITH HEAD

EDITH HEAD HAS WEATHERED THE RAGING STORMS AND BLEAK CALMS OF the Hollywood movie world for more than half a century. Responsible for over five hundred films, more than any other designer, she has demonstrated enormous flexibility and talent that has endeared her to actresses, producers, and directors alike. Her even-tempered, dependable approach to seemingly insurmountable problems has earned her the unqualified respect of her associates. She has costumed every type of film—from Westerns to drawing room comedies, monster movies to musicals, and biblical spectacles to kitchen-sink dramas—and by 1976, she had received eight Oscars and thirty-three nominations for the awards.

Though the birthdates on her passport and driver's license do not agree, Edith Head has acknowledged 1907 to be the year and San Bernardino, California, the place of her birth. Any records of the event and her family name were destroyed in a courthouse fire, so hers is the last word on the subject. The name Head is a remnant of her brief marriage in 1923 to Charles Head, the brother of an art-school chum named Betty. In her 1959 memoir, *The Dress Doctor*, the designer said it was "a marriage disrupted first by separation, then by Charles' illness, and eventually by his death."

During her childhood years, Edith lived with her mother and stepfather in an unpainted wooden house four lonely desert miles from Searchlight, Nevada.

The monotonous landscape was infested with rattlesnakes, scorpions, and tarantulas. Her exposure to such creatures taught her a principle that served her well in later years and in many situations: "Let them alone, they'll let you alone."

When Edith was twelve, her family moved back to Los Angeles, where they took an apartment downtown at Fourth Street and Grand. She soon discovered a nearby YWCA and became an enthusiastic gymnast, following a proclivity for sports that she continued to develop through the years.

When she entered the University of California at Berkeley, the painfully shy, five-foot-one-inch-tall Edith first put on the large dark glasses that later became her trademark. "I think they became a protective coloration from the beginning, so effective that I never had any sense of being part of the campus at all: I was a spectator," she said. At the university Edith majored in languages and developed a lasting interest in American Indian art and California's Spanish Colonial architecture. After graduating, she went to Stanford University for a master's in French. Her first job was teaching French at the Bishop School for Girls, an exclusive finishing school in La Jolla. This was followed by a teaching post at the Hollywood School for Girls in Los Angeles.

Most of Edith's pupils at the Hollywood School were the children of successful motion picture executives, among them Agnes, Cecilia, and Katherine De Mille. One afternoon the three girls invited their teacher to watch DeMille direct one of his famed spectacles at Paramount studios. She was bewildered, impressed, and excited by what she observed.

When asked by the school to teach an art class in addition to French, she enrolled in night classes at the Otis Art School. She later transferred to the Chouinard Art School, where she met Betty Head and was introduced to Betty's brother Charles.

In need of a job after her marriage to Charles Head dissolved, she answered a want ad for an artist in the *Los Angeles Times*. Her inquiry brought her an appointment with Howard Greer, Paramount's new chief costume designer, who needed an artist to sketch his designs for presentation to producers, directors, and stars. The drawings had to be done with flair to dramatize the designer's ideas and win approval. Most designers could sketch—some of them quite well—but the task was time consuming, so an assistant who could take over that chore was extremely valuable.

Aware that her drawing was not good enough to qualify her for such an important position, Head had borrowed some of her art school classmates' best drawings and paintings to show Greer. As he recalled in his autobiography: "A young girl, with a face like a pussy cat crossed with a Fujita drawing, appeared with a carpetbag full of sketches. There were architectural drawings, plans for interior decorations, magazine illustrations, and fashion designs. Struck dumb with admiration for anyone possessed of such diverse talents, I hired the gal on the spot. She came to work the next morning and looked out from under her bangs with the expression of a frightened terrier."

Head then admitted to Greer that she had borrowed her fellow students' work. "She might easily have saved her breath and her confession," Greer said

later, "for her talents soon proved she was more than worthy of the job." Hired as a junior designer for fifty dollars a week, about twice the amount of a teacher's salary, Head began a career with Paramount in which she would be its chief designer for twenty-nine years.

Head was noted for accepting every job she was given with enthusiasm. She painted butterfly wings on China silk for *Peter Pan*, decorated candy-cane and chocolate-marshmallow costumes for a Candy Ball sequence in De Mille's 1925 *The Golden Bed*, and colored Gloria Swanson's shoes. Continuing her night classes at art school, she was soon able to sketch adequately enough to satisfy both Greer and his apprentice designer, Travis Banton.

Head's earliest movie clothes were assembled from wardrobe department racks for Westerns and B movies. When Greer left Paramount in 1927 to open his own salon on Sunset Boulevard, Banton succeeded him as chief designer and made Head his assistant. Her first chance to design for a major star came when she costumed the tempestuous Lupe Velez as a poor señorita in *Wolf Song* (1929). The star was unhappy that Greer was not her designer, but Head won her confidence with her ability to speak Spanish and by promising her a spectacular dress for her love scene with Gary Cooper. Lupe could barely move once she was in the dress, but she was delighted with her gown, and ignored the remark of a critic who said, "If there hadn't been so much dress, there would have been more scene."

In 1933, when Banton left the studio for a buying spree in Paris, the responsibilities shouldered by his assistant included the costuming of Mae West in *She Done Him Wrong*. Although West's hourglass figure had already been well established, Head's gowns continued to play up the actress as the screen's super courtesan. With her pouter-pigeon bosom and generous hips relentlessly boned and corseted, West made movie history. "Tighter," West would gasp to her fitters, "tighter, there's nothing that could make me faint, honey."

During her career, Head often designed for West and when the star made a much-heralded return to the screen in *Myra Breckinridge* (1970), a clause in her contract stipulated Edith Head as the designer. As West told one writer, "Ah like Edith's things because they're allurin' without bein' vulga. Ya know, to be allurin' ya don't have ta look indecent—Ah like gowns that have just a little *insinuendo* about 'em." The contract also specified that only West could appear in the film wearing white clothes, one of her favorite devices for standing out in a scene.

Head also made fashion history with the sarong she created for Dorothy Lamour in *The Jungle Princess* (1936). By then Head was well established. The following year, in fact, she was credited with forty-nine Paramount movies, ranging from *Bulldog Drummond Comes Back* to *Waikiki Wedding*. Thus, when Banton left Paramount in 1938 to design at Universal Studios, Head was his logical successor. As a bonus, she received a trip to Europe, her first.

As Paramount's number one designer and the first woman to be solely responsible for a major studio's costume department, Head's new burdens were awesome. Her ascendancy came at a time when Hollywood's salad days were ending. Bread-and-butter B pictures, produced and rushed to distributors with breakneck speed became the fare that sustained an industry in need of financial nourishment during the aftermath of the Depression.

Low-budget blue-plate specials like *Tip-Off Girls* (1938), *The Gracie Allen Murder Case* (1939), *Comin' Round the Mountain* (1940), and *Henry Aldrich for President* (1941) did not offer a costume designer much opportunity to create Banton couture or Adrian fireworks, but they kept the front gates of the studio open. Working six days a week from 8:00 A.M. until midnight, and often on Sunday, Head costumed an average of thirty-five movies a year. It was normal for her to have the wardrobes for three or four films in process simultaneously, a stack of new scripts awaiting her consideration, and fittings scheduled at fifteen-minute intervals.

Sensitive to the needs and fears of the hardworking actresses who stood on her fitting platforms, Head rarely found it necessary to assert her rank as a film's designer. As she has said, a costume designer had to be "a combination of psychiatrist, artist, fashion designer, dressmaker, pincushion, historian, nursemaid, and purchasing agent." But all the understanding, willingness to compromise, and control she could muster proved of no avail in the case of Claudette Colbert. Only once, for Paramount's 1938 remake of *Zaza*, did Head design for that strong-willed French-born star.

Never one to mince words, the beautiful actress expressed in acerbic terms her displeasure at being miscast (she was quite right) as an 1890s soubrette in a French music hall. The truth was, Colbert felt uncomfortable playing period roles, and after *Zaza* only appeared in one other. Though Head's designs for *Zaza* answered a need for charming period clothes, Colbert felt they were too similar to those worn by Mae West in *She Done Him Wrong*, and she could not be persuaded otherwise. Her differences with Head were never reconciled, so in later Colbert films, Irene was brought in to design for the star, while Head was responsible for the other costumes.

While working on *Cradle Song* as Banton's assistant in 1933, Head had begun a long friendship with the art director Wiard (Bill) Ilhen. On September 8, 1940, dozens of pictures later, the couple eloped to Las Vegas in a friend's private plane. They were married in a civil ceremony performed by a judge who had been fetched by the pilot from playing slot machines in the Golden Nugget Cafe. They eventually settled into a rambling Spanish colonial style house, which they named Casa Ladera, off Coldwater Canyon in Los Angeles, and there Edith created a world that was far removed from studio problems.

The slickly feminine costumes that Head did for Barbara Stanwyck in 1941's *The Lady Eve* not only revealed the actress's potential in glamour roles, but established their designer as a professional with the know-how needed to discern and exploit star quality. Aware that Head's costumes had transformed a merely dependable actress into a potential box-office princess, Paramount gave Stanwyck's gowns full publicity. The star even praised Head in interviews, and from that time on insisted on having all future films (including those made at other studios) as well as her off-screen wardrobe created by the designer.

Though Head's movie clothes, such as the shoulder-tied boatneck she gave Audrey Hepburn in *Sabrina* (1954), have frequently been credited as fashion influences, Head has said that "anything I've done like that has been an accident: I'm not creating styles of fashion." Head's reed-slim clothes appeared unfashionable next to the New Look of Dior's bouffant skirts in 1947. "Ever since then, I've been a confirmed fence-sitter," says Head. "That's why I've been around so long."

Despite her almost constant association with movie design, Head has also been involved in numerous other fashion-oriented projects. In 1958 she created a garnet-velvet-and-gold-lamé gown and a cape embroidered in jewels for opera star Dorothy Kirsten to wear in *Tosca*. She has done women's uniforms for the Coast Guard and for Pan American Airlines, and designed printed fabrics. She taught a course in motion picture costume design at the University of Southern California and has written numerous articles and several books about her experiences as a Hollywood designer. She is also a noted lecturer and a frequent guest on television and radio talk shows and has toured the country promoting sewing patterns for Vogue Patterns. All such activities, however, Edith Head dismisses as mere perfunctory extracurricular activity. Designing movie costumes, she maintains, is her true calling.

Head's sketch for one of the controversial costumes she designed for Claudette Colbert in Zaza (Paramount, 1938)— and the finished product. Miss Colbert felt uncomfortable in period roles like this one.

Pink organdi

In May of 1966, control of Paramount passed to Gulf + Western, the conglomerate, and Head was out of a job for the first time in forty-odd years. But she had known her Paramount days were numbered, and, almost at once, she packed up and moved to Universal Studios, where she became resident costume designer. She returned only once to Paramount, in 1973, to design for Elizabeth Taylor in *Ash Wednesday*.

As an indication of what happened in the film industry from the forties to the seventies—Head designed thirty-four movies in 1941 alone, but during her first eight years at Universal her entire roster consisted of the same number of pro-

ductions. Edith Head is still active and has outlasted all others throughout an astonishing era in movie making.

Of course, anyone in such a prominent position is bound to have detractors. Head's fellow-designer Dorothy Jeakins has said, "Her work is extremely mediocre . . . [but] Edith deserves a lot of credit for hanging in there." Designer Raoul Pène du Bois, briefly a colleague at Paramount during the forties, less kindly noted that it was Head's assistants who developed costume designs from the minuscule thumbnail sketches she dashed off, and, in his opinion, she should not be considered a designer. On the other hand, Banton once told a friend that

Head was "the only one of us who could stick it out. . . . the last designer out there who really knows how to put together a movie costume." And Hal Wallis, for whom Head designed over sixty films, said "Edith has a great rapport with all the women she's dressed, which makes my life on the back lot a great deal easier." Stars like Mae West still remain loyal, too. For West's comeback in *Sextette* (1979) Head supplied her with the kind of stylish flamboyance so long associated with the actress. She considers Head "the only designer who can dress Mae West as Mae West . . . tight enough to show I'm a woman but loose enough to show I'm a lady."

Such pros and cons must be of little importance to Universal's designer. After working on literally hundreds of movies, she continues to practice her craft from her office at the end of the studio's Main Street. Eight shining gold Oscars decorate its entry; the first was for *The Heiress* in 1949, the second year that designers participated in the Academy Awards. Her other winning films were: *All About Eve* (1950), *Samson and Delilah* (1950), *A Place in the Sun* (1951), *Roman Holiday* (1953), *Sabrina* (1954), *The Facts of Life* (1960), and *The Sting* (1973).

At home, she swims and plays tennis with her husband of four decades. Unlike many of her predecessors, who ended up unhappily, Head enjoys the comforts bestowed by a long and successful career in Hollywood.

In a way, she is more truly a movie costume designer than many others who worked in Hollywood, because she had no ambition to design for any other medium. "When I design a dress," she once said, "it's done. I don't have to worry about how it sells. When a couturier finishes designing, he only just begins to worry."

Certainly the clothes that Head designs for herself—mostly suits and simple shirtmaker dresses of lightweight fabrics in muted colors of gray and beige—are not particularly striking. On a dare, she once appeared at a Hollywood party in a low-cut slinky beaded gown, sporting a pair of chandelier-shaped diamond earrings and a long feather boa. The outfit engendered such whoops of laughter from the other guests that Head never again attempted to emulate the kind of glamour she could conjure up for movie stars. One year her name appeared on a list of worst-dressed women, but it had no obvious effect on her wardrobe.

In a recent newspaper interview Head commented on the demise of Hollywood's famed years of extravagant production. "Then," she said, "a designer was as important as a star. When you said Garbo, you thought of Adrian; when you said Dietrich, you said Banton. The magic of an Adrian or Banton dress was part of the selling of a picture. Sets, costumes, and makeup just aren't considered the art forms they used to be."

The last of her kind, Edith Head has traveled the full range of Hollywood movie production and emerged as the grande dame of costume designers. She is a living reminder of what the movies used to be all about.

The costumes worn by Barbara Stanwyck in The Lady Eve *(1941) established Head's reputation.*

Veronica Lake in an Edith Head design for I Wanted Wings *(1940).*

The original caption for this forties publicity shot read: "Irene, executive designer for Metro-Goldwyn-Mayer, has been called the best-dressed designer in the country. She thinks a suit is the best choice for a business girl, because it is practical, smart and elegant at the same time. Here Irene wears a pale gray, lightweight suit, which features very interesting details on the jacket."

1901-1962

IRENE

When Irene (Irene Lentz-Gibbons) resigned from MGM in 1949, Louis B. Mayer sighed heavily and remarked, "So quiet she was—and expensive, Miss Don't-Melt-Ice-Cube." During her seven-year tenure at MGM only a minimum of discourse had passed between Mayer and his tall, husky-voiced designer. Sensitive and withdrawn, Irene had always gone about minding Mayer's business in her own manner. She was proud, often aloof, but a thorough professional with a touch of class that inhibited and bewildered Mayer.

Little is known about Irene's background except that she was born Irene Lentz in Brookings, South Dakota, in 1901, and found her way to Hollywood by 1925. That year she began work at MGM as an extra in the ballroom scene of *The Merry Widow*. While Mae Murray whirled around the floor in the arms of leading man John Gilbert, Irene was partnered by an aspiring actor named Walter Plunkett, who later became her codesigner at the studio. She later quipped, "Walter and I are really just a couple of disappointed movie extras."

After a brief stint as an extra, Irene enrolled in courses in music theory and composition at the University of Southern California. But a parallel interest in dress design prevailed, and she transferred to the Wolfe School of Design to study draping, drawing, and fashion design. A hard worker, Irene advanced rapidly and demonstrated unusual ability in designing apparel. She also developed a style of boldly signed fashion sketches that became her trademark.

Sometime around 1928, Irene married Richard Jones, about whom little else is known. Then, at the urging of her husband and friends, the designer opened a small dress shop on the UCLA campus. Almost at once it proved successful. Affluent students began availing themselves of Irene's svelte, original clothes, and one satisfied customer introduced the vivacious Mexican actress Lupe Velez to the shop.

Bored with the *Rio Rita* look Hollywood designers inevitably gave her, Velez was surprised and delighted by an impeccably tailored silk coat-and-dress outfit created by Irene. Velez in turn recommended Irene to her friend and compatriot, Dolores Del Rio, who promptly ordered six dresses, two of them romantic evening gowns of the kind that would make Irene famous.

With the sudden death of her husband only two years after they were married, Irene closed her shop and left for Europe. She toured England and the Continent and then lived in Paris for several months, where she viewed the collections of the couturiers and pored over fashion plates at museums. As with most designers who visit that city, it had an enduring influence on her art.

After several months abroad, Irene returned to Los Angeles and opened a second salon. She did so well that she was forced to find larger quarters in 1932. By then, many movie celebrities had found their way to her door, and the window displays of her shop became famous for their originality and elegance. They so impressed an executive of the fashionable Bullock's Wilshire department store that he offered Irene a generous contract to design for and head Bullock's Custom Salon. After some hesitancy, Irene accepted, and in 1935 full-page advertisements for her designs for Bullock's began appearing in *Vogue, Harper's Bazaar,* and *Town and Country*.

Within months, any garment bearing an Irene label was an indication that its wearer was a person of taste, position, and means. In 1935, a low price for a custom-designed Irene evening gown was $450. In Paris, a woman could be fitted in a gown of similar quality for about two hundred dollars. "Expensive," was the word that Louis B. Mayer would later moan in regard to Irene.

Irene's first screen credit had been shared with Howard Greer in RKO's 1932 film version of Philip Barry's play *The Animal Kingdom,* with Ann Harding and Leslie Howard. This was followed by *Flying Down to Rio* (1933), an RKO love-among-the-clouds musical with Dolores Del Rio and Fred Astaire. Del Rio, a private client of Irene's, insisted that the studio hire the designer on a free-lance basis to create her costumes.

As a successful designer of the personal wardrobes of many of Hollywood's most glittering stars, Irene received more and more commissions to dress them on camera as well as off. Claudette Colbert, Rosalind Russell, Irene Dunne, Loretta Young, Constance Bennett, and Ginger Rogers all occupied front chairs at Irene's openings at Bullock's, and Irene's name began to appear in movie credits as codesigner with leading studio costumers.

The shared billings, coupled with Irene's rather distant manner and impeccably groomed appearance (which a number of staff designers interpreted as being too grand), often caused resentment. Irene and her staff were never known to come onto a set without wearing immaculate white gloves and suitable hats.

Irene's sketch and the suit worn by Joan Crawford in They All Kissed the Bride *(Columbia, 1942).*

After Adrian left MGM in 1942, Irene became executive designer under a seven-year contract. She also had an indirect link to the studio through her marriage to Eliot Gibbons, the brother of MGM's brilliant art director, Cedric Gibbons. That relationship led to all sorts of unfavorable gossip about influence peddling, which certainly did not improve Irene's image. But, in any event, the world of the movie studio did not really suit her temperament.

In her role as chief designer for the studio, Irene had to deal with other executives, producers, directors, cameramen, movie stars, and publicity people. She was more involved with administrative duties and budgets than with designing the kind of soigné clothes that were her main interest. The work load was immense and the shortages of materials and labor brought on by the war were added problems.

Nonetheless, Irene stayed for seven years at MGM, and was aided primarily by Kay Dean and Marion Herwood Keyes, as well as J. Arlington Valles, who costumed the male stars. During that period, she was credited as costume designer for fifty-six films, though she did not actually do them all herself. Irene

215

lacked a knowledge of period clothes and turned to free-lance help for the typically garish show-girl trappings needed in MGM's money-making musicals. The Russian Mme Karinska was brought in for Ingrid Bergman's intricate Victorian clothes in *Gaslight* (1944), and she remained at MGM to create the fanciful costumes worn by Marlene Dietrich in *Kismet,* though Irene received credit for them. Such erroneous attributions, although legal under Irene's contract, were sore points with other designers and increased their resentment of her. Another problem grew out of her position as final arbiter in all matters of costume design, which led to many arguments over the fine points of an outfit.

Although a great number of MGM movies, such as *Swing Shift Maisie* (1943) and *Son of Lassie* (1945), were less than inspiring for a designer of Irene's caliber, others called upon all of her resources. Some of the memorable ones were *Mrs. Parkington* (1944), *Weekend at the Waldorf* (1945), *The Postman Always Rings Twice* (1946), *State of the Union* (1948), and *B.F.'s Daughter* (1948), which earned an Academy Award nomination for best costume design.

In 1947, Mayer granted Irene permission to design for a wholesale outlet. It was exceptional for a studio head to allow a designer to work outside home ground, but Irene's contract was almost up and Mayer had no intention of renewing it. Twenty-five leading department stores financed the venture and held exclusive rights to Irene's designs. It was the first time that the apparel of a prestigious American designer was made available to department-store buyers in small cities, and the experiment met with instant success. From Seattle to Pittsburgh, women crowded Irene's boutique-salons in their hometown department stores, eager to be identified with the designer who dressed Irene Dunne, Barbara Stanwyck, Greer Garson, and Loretta Young.

After Irene left MGM she continued to design personal wardrobes for a large number of stars, but only occasionally returned to dressing them for the screen. She costumed Loretta Young in *Key to the City* (1950), and Doris Day in *Midnight Lace* (1960), which earned her another Academy Award nomination. Day also wore Irene clothes in her successful film comedy *Lover Come Back* (1962). Irene's last screen credit was for *A Gathering of Eagles,* finished just before her suicide in 1962.

As MGM's executive designer, Irene had not generally fraternized with studio personnel, but in private life she was well liked and a good friend of many Hollywood celebrities. Among them she could be warm, charming, and a gracious hostess, and it was with genuine concern that her friends watched helplessly as the designer grew dependent on alcohol to escape from her anxiety-filled existence. For long periods she was separated from her husband, and there were rumors of a hopeless love affair with Gary Cooper that led to bouts of depression bordering on despair. Whether such a liaison actually existed or not, it became obvious that her personal problems were overwhelming.

With all her other disappointments, Irene also suffered the failure of not having succeeded as much in costuming for films as she had in custom and mass-produced design. In confiding her feelings to Travis Banton, she referred to her position at MGM as "a terrible mistake." "There was nothing I could say," Banton observed. "She was right."

Classic soft, flowing designs like this one worn by Rosalind Russell were Irene's hallmark.

Irene was the first prestigious American designer to have boutique-salons in department stores around the country.

Orry-Kelly with June Haver.

1897-1964

ORRY-KELLY

ORRY-KELLY WAS HEAD COSTUME DESIGNER FOR WARNER BROTHERS FROM 1932 to 1944; and with Adrian at MGM and Travis Banton at Paramount, he formed Hollywood's famed triumvirate of costumers in the thirties. Years ago, Jack Warner, production head of the studio, reminisced to me about Kelly: "I used to tell Kelly he should have been a prizefighter or gone into vaudeville," he said. "He could be trouble, loved the spotlight, and was stubborn as hell. When he had too many drinks he'd get mean, start swearing and throwing punches. But he could be a damn nice guy when he wanted to be. His costumes had the one thing I always insisted on in everything—*quality;* you see, there was *quality* there. No one else could touch them in that."

Warner also described the fifty or so times Kelly quit: They would yell at each other, Kelly would storm out, slam the door, and tell everyone what a bastard Warner was. But he always came back, and for years Warner let him stay.

He was born John Orry Kelly on December 1, 1897, in Kiama, Australia. His parents were middle-class Irish emigrants. His unusual middle name, selected by his mother, was inspired by the Orry carnation, a variety that flourished in her garden. The hyphenation began as a typing error in his first Warner Brothers contract, but it seemed to lend the name an air of distinction, so it was retained. Among friends, though, the designer was called Jack, and his bar buddies, who included Errol Flynn, nicknamed him Killer.

While he was still in his teens, Kelly's family moved to Sydney. In those days the city had the vigorous atmosphere of a boom town. It also had such amenities as theater performances by English and American stock companies. Once Kelly discovered the stage, he set his heart on being an actor. He began to study voice, and, on his own, emulated the soft-shoe routines of the hoofers who were the favorites of the Saturday-night audiences in Sydney's downtown music halls. Kelly also attended art classes, developing painting and drawing skills that had been apparent since childhood.

To earn a living Kelly worked at a variety of jobs, including that of mural painter for restaurants and shops. By 1923, when he was twenty-six, Kelly had saved enough money to book passage to New York. He then announced to his incredulous friends that he would seek fame as a song-and-dance man on the Broadway stage—and perhaps become a movie star.

Kelly joined the stream of young actors seeking a break in New York as they poured through the offices of producers and agents. But after grueling weeks of interviews, auditions, readings, and tryouts, the once-confident young man faced the grim reality of having to put aside his theatrical ambitions and find another means of support.

Jobs were scarce, so Kelly worked as waiter, salesclerk, and hotel clerk before exploiting his ability in decorative painting. He prepared a portfolio of designs for murals and was surprised when it brought him a number of commissions from department stores and restaurants. Though his film design career diverted him away from painting, Kelly, like other costume designers, always remained a "Sunday painter." In later years his pictures decorated the homes of a number of his movie-star friends, and many were exhibited and sold in Hollywood and New York. Ann Warner hung a number of his impressionistic works in the Pasadena mansion she decorated so superbly, and Marion Davies, in typical grand manner, once bought nine pictures at one of Kelly's Hollywood exhibitions.

Encouraged by the early response to his artistic efforts, Kelly tried his hand at portraits and soon found his charcoal-drawn likenesses were well received by his theater friends in New York. Included among his new acquaintances in the city was a good-looking, energetic young English actor named Archibald Leach, who was bound for Hollywood. The two became good friends and Archie, rechristened Cary Grant by Paramount, was later instrumental in introducing Kelly to Warner Brothers.

Kelly's break actually came when his murals were brought to the attention of a stage director, who hired him to design several sets and a number of costumes for a revue. The production was far from a smashing success, but Kelly's contribution did not go unnoticed by other directors and managers. Before long he enjoyed modest acclaim, and his stage aspirations were transformed into a desire to design for the theater. As a vestige of his early ambitions, Kelly could always be counted on to entertain at Hollywood parties with his neat soft-shoe routines and the side-splitting rendition of the early Rodgers and Hart song "I'd Like to Poison Ivy" that he had used for his auditions.

Kelly landed his first movie job in the New York art department of Fox productions. For a brief time there he created the fancy borders that appeared around titles in silent movies. But he had also begun to design costumes for various vaudeville shows at the Palace Theatre. He dressed Nora Bayes, "The Greatest Single Woman Comedienne in the World," and Blossom Seeley, "Songstress and Artiste." On the dramatic side, he also created several costumes for the illustrious Ethel Barrymore. In spite of his other talents, Kelly quickly realized his future lay in costume design, and he left New York for Hollywood, where opportunities seemed greater.

Within a week of his arrival in Los Angeles, Kelly's old friend Cary Grant presented the designer's portfolio to an executive at First National Films (later bought by Warner Brothers). Not only was Kelly offered a job as wardrobe assistant, but he was also assured that if his designs received the blessing of First National's top stars, Kay Francis and Ruth Chatterton, a contract as studio designer would be forthcoming.

When the chic, often haughty Miss Chatterton raved about Kelly's sketches, and Miss Francis added her approval, Kelly was signed on. His first film was Darryl Zanuck's *The Rich Are Always with Us* (1932), in which Chatterton starred and Bette Davis was the blonde ingenue.

That was the beginning of one of the great actress-designer combinations. Like Garbo and Adrian, and Dietrich and Banton, Davis and Orry-Kelly exemplified artists who acted as catalysts upon each other and together produced extraordinary work. Kelly was able to recognize Davis's need for costumes that would strongly support her dramatic roles with as few distracting encumbrances as possible.

Only once in the fourteen years he costumed Davis at Warner Brothers did Orry-Kelly attempt merely to glamorize her, and he did it at the insistence of Jack Warner. Davis appeared in *Fashions of 1934* wearing sultry clothes, heavy makeup, and sophisticated hairdos. When she saw the completed film, the horrified actress raged at her image and made it clear beyond a doubt that she would never again allow Warner to tamper with her roles. Kelly agreed with her. "I dressed her for the character she had to play," he later said. "She was an actress who had a job to do and it was mine to help her do it."

Kelly's period costumes for Davis were especially outstanding because he always strove to produce effective, dramatic garments based on solid historic research. Some of his most notable were done for *The Old Maid* (1939), *The Private Lives of Elizabeth and Essex* (1939), and *The Little Foxes* (1941). For *Mr. Skeffington* (1944) Kelly created forty costumes for Miss Davis that spanned several decades of her character's life. Though he had by then left Warners for good, at Davis's insistence Kelly costumed her for Miss Moffat in the 1945 *The Corn Is Green*.

Other actresses dressed by Kelly include Glenda Farrell, Fay Wray, Margaret Lindsay, and Joan Blondell. He served them all well, though his strong personality often sparked flare-ups in the wardrobe fitting rooms. Kelly was apt to forget such clashes as quickly as they occurred, however, and his flattering costumes earned him the forbearance of many leading ladies.

Kelly's clothes were always made of the finest fabrics and were hand finished. Among his hallmarks were intricate decorative detailing that encompassed the

Studio sketch, 1932.

A design for Kay Francis in One Way Passage *(Warner Brothers, 1932).*

narrowest pipings, fine pleating, openwork embroidery, trapunto, crocheted lace, and exquisite hand-painted designs.

Socially, Kelly was a popular figure in Hollywood, a regular at parties and noted for his wit. He was also a good friend of Hearst's love, Marion Davies, who in turn was close to Hearst's powerful columnist Louella Parsons. Quite likely Jack Warner would have dispensed with Kelly much sooner had Parsons not contrived to prevent the newspapers from having a field day with the designer's drinking problem. Grateful for her help, Kelly was always available when Louella needed a new gown, and he would fit her himself. One Christmas he even sent her a magnificent chinchilla evening wrap.

Louella was dressed by Kelly for her part in Warner Brothers' lavish musical *Hollywood Hotel* (1937). It is said that Jack Warner cast Parsons in the film to flatter her into giving his stars frequent mention in her column. Kelly also stood himself in good stead with the columnist by bedecking Lolly's ample bosom with $165,000 worth of rented diamonds and emeralds.

Louella proved to be a good and faithful friend. In one instance, she rushed to Kelly's rescue after he had had a few too many at a party in Beverly Hills. Kelly had insulted the host, staggered into the street, and commanded what he thought was a taxi to stop. The taxi turned out to be a police car and the designer was driven off in a rage to the local precinct. A witness to his plight, Louella fished a thousand dollars out of her purse for bail and dispatched her husband, "Docky," to the police station in her Rolls-Royce to rescue the hapless designer. In another instance when Kelly was in need of money, Louella organized an exhibition of his paintings in Beverly Hills and watched him like a mother hen to make sure he didn't overdo it at the opening-night party.

By the 1940s, Kelly's position at Warners had grown tenuous. Although the clothes he gave Ingrid Bergman in *Casablanca* kindled a weak reconciliation between him and his hard-hitting boss, Jack Warner, everyone knew it would only be a matter of time before they would be at odds again. A final clash between them was temporarily averted when Kelly was drafted into the army in the middle of *Old Acquaintance* (1943). The film was already in turmoil because of the rivalry of the film's two stars, Bette Davis and Miriam Hopkins; Miss Hopkins insisted that Kelly had given Davis better costumes, and Davis, the studio's top moneymaker, flaunted her powerful position. Kelly only added to the fracas with frequent outbursts of temper: On one occasion he stomped on a bonnet that Hopkins had obtained on her own and had sent to wardrobe together with a crude sketch of the hat with a larger taffeta bow.

While he was in the service, Kelly's design duties were assumed by Leah Rhodes, one of several contract designers at Warners, who finished *Old Acquaintance* in good form. Not long afterward, when Kelly suddenly reappeared at Warners—discharged from the service for drinking—he admitted to friends that he could "read the handwriting on the wall." But, in spite of himself, his old temper tantrums and drinking resumed, giving Jack Warner good reason to dismiss him. Louella personally called on Warner and told him she would seek medical help for Kelly, but Warner refused to budge. However, it was Bette

Although Orry-Kelly did his best, Bette Davis's appearance in Warners' Fashions of 1934 caused her to shriek with rage and swear never again to allow costumes to become the major support of her highly individualistic performances. Even the tufted-satin background in this photograph seems to abet the unfortunate effort to gild the perennial and glowing lily of the silver screen.

Davis who had the final word. She demanded that Kelly design her costumes for *Mr. Skeffington.*

Meanwhile, in 1943, Kelly accepted a job at Twentieth Century-Fox for thirty thousand dollars a year. He stayed there until 1947, designing for Darryl Zanuck's star Betty Grable, among others; from 1950 to 1964, Kelly free-lanced for Fox, MGM, United Artists, and Warner Brothers, and during that period won three Academy Awards. The first he shared with Irene Sharaff and Walter Plunkett for MGM's *An American In Paris* (1951); the other two were for *Les Girls* (1957) and *Some Like It Hot* (1959). Other notable films of these later years were

Ava Gardner in one of Orry-Kelly's last costumes, for Fifty-Five Days at Peking *(Allied Artists, 1963).*

A Majority of One (1961), *Gypsy* (1962), *Sweet Bird of Youth* (1962), *Fifty-Five Days at Peking* (1963), and Kelly's last films—*Irma La Douce* (1963) and *The Cool of Day* (1964)—completed before he died in 1964.

Unfortunately, the autobiography that Kelly had been working on at the time of his death was incomplete. His story was certainly one of Hollywood's most colorful, and his work was extraordinary. As Jack Warner said of his costumes, "They had quality—no one else could touch them in that."

Walter Plunkett chats with Katharine Hepburn while she rests on a leaning board during the filming of MGM's Sea of Grass *(1947). Plunkett was Hepburn's favorite costume designer, and they did many films together.*

WALTER PLUNKETT

WALTER PLUNKETT IS GENERALLY ACKNOWLEDGED TO BE HOLLYWOOD'S foremost designer of period costumes, and is probably best known for his work in *Gone With the Wind*. Looking at the film, which made Vivien Leigh *the* movie heroine of her time, Plunkett has said: "I don't think it was my best work, or even the biggest thing I ever did. There were more designs for *Singin' in the Rain, Raintree County*, and *How the West Was Won*." But the green velvet, hoop-skirted gown that Scarlett fashioned from the portieres in her mother's dining room was probably the most famous costume in the history of motion pictures.

Born in 1902 in Oakland, California, Plunkett grew up there and studied law at the University of California in Berkeley. He joined a small theater group on campus and developed an interest in acting. By the time he was ready to graduate, Plunkett was so thoroughly wrapped up with the stage that his father gave him a ticket to New York. After playing small parts in two Broadway shows and taking a turn on the vaudeville circuit, Plunkett returned to California to try his luck in Hollywood.

His screen debut was as a "dress" extra, waltzing Irene Lentz around a glittering ballroom in the *The Merry Widow*. A few more bit parts followed, but Plunkett needed something more substantial and finally accepted a position in the wardrobe department at FBO studios. FBO specialized in Westerns, two-reel

Plunkett's sketch for a gown of mousseline embroidered with morning glories over blue taffeta, with a changeable lavender/green taffeta bodice, designed for Elizabeth Taylor in MGM's 1957 Raintree County. *This film required even more elaborate costumes than had* Gone With the Wind.

comedies, and cops-and-robbers chase thrillers. A few months after Plunkett joined the studio, its name was changed to RKO and he was made its costume designer. Soon the studio was planning more ambitious projects, and Plunkett was asked to set up a design department. He hired seamstresses, tailors, and cutters for his workrooms and started costuming such potboilers as *Ain't Love Funny* (1926), *Clancy's Kosher Wedding* (1927), and *Wizard of the Saddle* (1928). Although he had no formal training, Plunkett turned out costume after costume, and by 1931 was fully ready for his first important movie: *Cimarron*, starring Irene Dunne and directed by Wesley Ruggles.

Cimarron gave Plunkett an opportunity to create period clothes, and he immediately demonstrated his strength in that area. The following year he did a few insignificant films, and then in 1933 he was given *Flying Down to Rio*, the first film in which Fred Astaire danced with Ginger Rogers. The film was made famous by their dancing to the pseudo-Latin rhythms of Vincent Youman's "Carioca," and it featured scantily clad chorus girls doing a routine on the wings of airplanes high above the bay of Rio. Plunkett would later say it was "total absurdity"; but the film made Astaire and Rogers into a new Hollywood gold mine and Walter Plunkett into a designer of more than mere promise. That same year Plunkett also costumed Katharine Hepburn as Jo in *Little Women*, and for two other films. It was the beginning of a long and mutually satisfying alliance with Miss Hepburn.

By 1935, Plunkett's responsibilities at RKO had almost exceeded his endurance. To make things worse, he was assigned to many films of little consequence with few artistic rewards. Of the twenty-three movies done by Plunkett that year, only *Alice Adams* and *Sylvia Scarlett* (both starring Katharine Hepburn) and *The Informer* seemed worthy of him. He later complained: "I was not only the designer but manager of the wardrobe department. I had the payroll, the hiring and firing of seamstresses, and the budget to look after, plus doing my own sketches and clothes. I had no contract, was given no screen credit half the time, was earning seventy-five dollars a week, and they were giving the best pictures to Bernard Newman" (another designer at the studio). Exhausted and disgusted, Plunkett resigned and left for New York, where he accepted an offer to design for a Seventh Avenue dress manufacturer.

After a year's sabbatical, Plunkett was lured back to RKO at the request of Katharine Hepburn to create her costumes for Maxwell Anderson's *Mary of Scotland*. Hepburn's choice was a wise one, and Plunkett's superb designs brought him new appreciation from studio chieftains. He decided to stay in Hollywood, but on his own terms, as a free-lance designer who could pick and choose his films. From that point in his career until his retirement in 1966, Plunkett dressed many of the greatest stars in some of Hollywood's most ambitious and successful movies.

In 1939, Plunkett was signed to costume Ginger Rogers in *The Story of Vernon and Irene Castle*, a film that from the beginning was fraught with difficulties. Irene Castle, who was in comfortable and fashionable retirement, insisted on having approval of script, cast, direction, and costumes and was not at all pleased with the choice of Rogers. Mrs. Castle and Plunkett generally disagreed on the designs, and when they *did* reach some kind of accord, Rogers usually lodged her own complaints. To make matters worse, the manner in which Mrs. Castle expressed her disdain for costumes that displeased her could be devastating. She once rejected a dress with the observation that it looked too "Plunketty." The final costume credits were divided between Walter Plunkett and Edward Stevenson with the added line: "Miss Rogers' Gowns, Irene Castle." *Gone With the Wind*, which Plunkett did in the same year for independent producer David O. Selznick, balanced that disaster.

Active for forty years, Plunkett was credited with over 260 films, but too many of them represented shameful wastes of his talent. Some of the better ones were: *A Song to Remember* (Columbia, 1945, with Travis Banton, starring Merle Oberon), *Green Dolphin Street* (MGM, 1947, with Valles, starring Lana Turner), *The Sea of Grass* and *Song of Love* (MGM, 1947, both starring Katharine Hepburn), *Madame Bovary* (MGM, 1949, with Valles, starring Jennifer Jones), *Adam's Rib* (MGM, 1949, again starring Hepburn), *Summer Stock* (MGM, 1950, with Helen Rose, starring Judy Garland), *An American In Paris* (MGM, 1951, for which, costuming Nina Foch and Leslie Caron, among others in the cast, he shared an Academy Award with Irene Sharaff and Orry-Kelly), *Kiss Me Kate* (MGM, 1953, starring Kathryn Grayson and Ann Miller), and *7 Brides for 7 Brothers* (MGM, 1954, starring Jane Powell).

Perhaps Plunkett received too little attention from studio publicists because he was so mild mannered. He may also have suffered from working as a freelancer without the continued support of a major studio. In any event, he was greatly admired among his peers and even had he done nothing else, his fame would rest secure on one film alone, *Gone With the Wind*. As he reportedly said, "That picture will go on forever." And so will the artistry of its costume designer.

Walter Plunkett's full-skirted day dress of tiered linen edged with handworked lattice perfectly suited the wistful Jennifer Jones as Madame Bovary (1949).

The caption from this 1954 MGM publicity photo reads: "ALL-AMERICAN ROSE . . . is Hel-en to her friends and an Academy award-winning fashion designer at M-G-M. Born and reared in Chicago, Miss Rose took to dressing dolls at an early age and is still at it. . . . In her all-beige office where she meets daily with glamorous stars, Helen Rose inspects sketches of her costume designs."

HELEN ROSE

HELEN ROSE, LIKE HER PEERS EDITH HEAD AND IRENE, IS ONE OF THE RARE women to have been named chief costume designer for a major Hollywood studio—a title reserved almost exclusively for men. During twenty-three years devoted to dressing the movies' good, bad, and beautiful stars, Rose herself achieved fame as a leading lady of Hollywood costume design. Her clothes were elegant and understated but innovative, and they always looked natural in spite of their theatrical use.

In her amusing and warmly written book, *Just Make Them Beautiful*, Rose recorded her rise to movie fame. She was born around 1908 (she refuses to tell her true age) to middle-class parents, who lived on Chicago's South Side. By the age of six she had already expressed an interest in fashion and loved to scrawl crayon drawings of ladies in flowered hats. This interest was encouraged by the girl's mother, who had been a seamstress in a garment factory. When mother and daughter spent summer afternoons in the park, Helen, at her mother's urging, would sketch the fashions they saw around them.

Such artistic endeavor did not sit well with the girl's father, however. Though he represented a lithograph company that reproduced popular works of art, he was convinced that "all artists end up drunks or starving in a garret." Helen's mother placated him with the assurance that their daughter would become a dress designer. "I think she would have encouraged me in anything to keep me away from a sewing machine," Helen later said.

Until she was fourteen, Helen diligently studied the typing and shorthand her father believed were essential to a young woman facing the business world of the twenties. At last, however, he capitulated to his daughter's pleading and permitted her to leave high school and enroll in the Chicago Academy of Fine Arts.

At first Helen joined her classmates in attempts to imitate the imaginative, meticulously detailed drawings of Erté, the most emulated designer-illustrator of the time. But she simply wasn't able to express her own ideas in someone else's style. Her drawings were certainly no threat to Erté, but they were original enough to catch the sharp eye of "a very classy gentleman named Mr. Lester," who owned the Lester Costume Company.

Every year, Lester made a point of viewing student exhibitions at Chicago's art schools, hopeful of finding talents that would serve the needs of his workshop at Wabash Avenue and Lake Street. After scanning an art show at Helen's school, Lester judged her work the best of the lot and offered her an opportunity to concoct "girlie" costumes for vaudeville and nightclub extravaganzas, his company's particular forte. Ever mindful that talent ought to be rewarded in tangible terms, the dapper Lester tossed caution aside and agreed to compensate the designer at the rate of 37½ cents an hour.

The ecstatic Helen couldn't resist. She piled her long hair on top of her head, dressed in an altered outfit borrowed from an aunt, put on a pair of dangling earrings to disguise her obvious youth, and set out for the Loop and a new career as a costume designer. Not even her studio dampened her enthusiasm; no larger than a cell, it was situated so near the El that the cubicle shook violently each time a train roared by. But Helen's joy at endlessly turning out sketches for her wily boss's customers seemed boundless, and any lingering doubts about her occupation soon vanished.

From the outset Helen had to develop tremendous versatility. For one show she transformed sixteen chorus girls into an assortment of dancing cupcakes. For another she turned a group of busty blondes disguised as a bunch of spring daffodils into fiery shimmy dancers. Lester's customers liked what they saw, and, after a few weeks' work, Helen was told she would henceforth receive forty-two cents an hour. At last a full-fledged designer, Helen notified her parents of another change: Her hair would be bobbed.

Mr. Lester's best customer was a producer and booking agent named Ernie Young. A sometime comedian, Young dressed in a manner more appropriate to vaudeville than Michigan Boulevard. He wore a fur-collared coat, pearl gray spats, and his hand flashed a pinky ring that he swore had a genuine diamond. With the typical modesty of a theatrical agent, Young chose to identify himself simply as "the Ziegfeld of the Middle West." Like his idol in New York, he firmly believed that the key to successful show-business was a stable of long-legged fillies whose modesty was tantalizingly protected by strategically placed rhinestone pasties and tiny triangles of jeweled fabric, and Helen's costumes looked pretty good to him. Young soon presented her with a proposition that was too good to refuse. He fancied Lester's young discovery as the designer, sketcher, and workroom supervisor of the costume company he was starting, and he offered her fifty dollars a week, twice her current pay.

Helen's first assignment at Young's new costume house was to clothe the show girls for a production inaugurating the Chez Pierre, a nightclub on Chicago's Near North Side. On opening night Helen's set of provocative harlequin costumes, made primarily of a few carefully placed patches of satin, came apart in a tantalizing manner under the stress of the girls' strutting. The audience, believing it was part of the act, applauded wildly, and the costumes were lauded by the press as some of the most original ever seen in the Windy City. In celebration, the exuberant Rose bought herself a raccoon coat at Marshall Field. As she remembers, "The timid little moth had become a butterfly."

She also had a suitor, nicknamed Babe, who came from an affluent family on the South Side and drove a Stutz. He gave her a large book of colored costume plates, which always remained in her library, as well as a copy of *Indian Love Lyrics*, and he encouraged her work. Unfortunately, about six months after their meeting, Babe's picture appeared below glaring headlines on the front page of a Chicago paper with a young man he had introduced to Helen as his "best friend, 'Dickie.'" Their real names were Nathan Leopold, Jr., and Richard Loeb, and they were accused of kidnapping and murder.

Helen worked three years for Ernie Young, learning every aspect of the costume design business. Under the supervision of Ernie's wife, Pearl, the company made money, and with its success, Helen's reputation as a theatrical designer grew steadily. Then the stock market crashed, and Young became seriously ill and had to give up the business.

Helen found a job designing for another costume house, but she soon became dissatisfied with it and joined a small costumer's on State Street that specialized in chiffon ball gowns. For some reason Helen's employer loathed the jaunty Ernie Young passionately, and expressed her contempt for anyone who had ever been associated with him. She assigned Helen to a completely isolated drawing table hidden behind a screen in the corner of the showroom and insulted and scorned her with almost monotonous regularity. But Helen was well paid, and, more important, she learned the art of designing with chiffon, a talent that later distinguished her among other movie designers. The fashion salon that she eventually established on her own was called the House of Chiffon.

A clash with her employer was inevitable. When it came, Helen quit and joined her parents in their moving to the West Coast. In Los Angeles Helen found work in a costume company owned by Walter and Ethel Israel, on Hollywood Boulevard. It supplied wardrobes for film companies, and Helen's first movie costumes were commissioned for D. W. Griffith's *Abraham Lincoln*, starring Walter Huston and Una Merkel.

In 1930, Helen married Harry Rose, whom she had met just before leaving Chicago, and from that time on she was known professionally as Helen Rose. (Like Edith Head, she prefers not to reveal her family name.) By 1931, Helen had begun to design costumes for Fanchon and Marco's "vest pocket" dance versions of popular musicals. A number of promising unknowns who later became stars in the movies appeared in those modest but tasteful productions. Among them were Bing Crosby, Betty Grable, Judy Garland, Martha Raye, and Mae West. Fanchon also headed a dance school for children, and it was there that Rose first met Ann Miller, Shirley Temple, and Jane Withers, all of whom she costumed later on.

Before long, a number of Helen's sketches were shown to Rita Kaufman, the supervising designer at Fox Studios, and she was offered a job designing for the movies at $125 a week. Helen accepted immediately, but after only four months Kaufman left Fox and her staff was dismissed. The stint left Rose "starry-eyed," but she did not attempt to continue as a movie designer. Instead, she began a long and highly successful tenure as costumer for Shipstad and Johnson's elaborate Ice Follies.

It was not until 1942 that Rose once again found herself on a Hollywood sound stage. At the behest of Fanchon, she was hired by Twentieth Century-Fox as musical coordinator to provide spectacular clothes for *Coney Island; Hello, Frisco, Hello;* and *Stormy Weather* (all, 1943). Working feverishly, Rose costumed all three films in three months and did so well that Fox invited her to stay on as their designer. Though flattered, she returned to her job with the Follies.

After Adrian left MGM in 1941, Louis B. Mayer had trouble finding a replacement. He tried Howard Shoup, Kalloch, and Irene, and then instructed his agents to hire Helen Rose, whose costumes he had seen and liked. At first Rose hesitated to join what Hedda Hopper called Looie's Zoo, but the offer of $750 a week was irresistible. On September 1, 1943, Helen signed as a staff designer with MGM.

By 1947, Rose had designed only four films for MGM: *Ziegfeld Follies* (with Irene Sharaff, 1944; released 1946), *The Harvey Girls, Two Sisters from Boston*, and *Till the Clouds Roll By* (all three 1946). Then she was assigned the musical numbers for *The Unfinished Dance*; Irene was to design the other clothes in the film. Joe Pasternak, the director, made little secret of his preference for Rose's designs, and a conference was called in the front office. The lion roared, and shortly thereafter, Irene announced she was leaving MGM to open her own couture business. From 1947 to 1949, Helen Rose designed costumes for twenty-three films at MGM, and by the time she retired from the studio in 1966, the count had increased to over two hundred.

Rose's down-to-earth, warm personality quickly won her the backing of Jerry Mayer, studio manager and brother of L.B., who welcomed her into the studio's executive circle and introduced her to the delicious chicken soup (made from a recipe of Mama Mayer's) that was a required daily item on the commissary menu. With such royal patronage, Rose was firmly ensconced as chief costume designer, and it wasn't long before L.B. was calling her "my sweetheart Rose."

During her years at MGM, Rose dressed an astounding roster of stars, including Lana Turner, Ava Gardner, Elizabeth Taylor, Grace Kelly, Deborah Kerr, Cyd Charisse, Jane Powell, and Esther Williams. And the variety of films she did costumes for is equally impressive. They include: *Good News* (1947), *Words*

Helen Rose meeting with Lena Horne in 1946.

and Music (1948), *That Midnight Kiss* (1949), *The Great Caruso* (1950), *The Merry Widow* (1952), *The Bad and the Beautiful* (1952), *Torch Song* (1953), *The Glass Slipper* (1954), *The Swan* (1956), *High Society* (1956), *Tea and Sympathy* (1956), *Silk Stockings* (1957), *Cat on a Hot Tin Roof* (1958), *It Started with a Kiss* (1959), *Butterfield 8* (1960), and *The Honeymoon Machine* (1961). She received two Academy Awards, for *The Bad and the Beautiful* and for *I'll Cry Tomorrow* (1955) and eight Academy Award nominations.

Rose's costumes were an integral part of the on-screen glamour images of Elizabeth Taylor, Grace Kelly, and Lana Turner. She gave them a soft, practical, up-to-date look that reflected the contemporary young American suburbanite. As a mark of her talent, both Elizabeth Taylor and Grace Kelly were wed in

Design for Grace Kelly in The Swan *(MGM, 1956).*

Grace Kelly dancing with Louis Jourdan in a scene from The Swan.
Copyright 1956 Loew's Incorporated Inc.

Helen Rose gowns. For her marriage to Nicky Hilton, Liz wore an adaptation of the satin dress Rose had designed for her in *Father of the Bride* (1950). Princess Grace's dress, made of French lace embroidered over pale rose taffeta, was a gift from MGM, and it has been preserved in the permanent collection of the costume department at the Philadelphia Museum of Art.

In 1958, Helen opened her own private business, where she continued to dress the luscious ladies of Hollywood, off the screen. Her expensive ready-to-wear was also sold under franchise in exclusive department stores and specialty shops across the country. Among Rose's largest buyers were Bonwit Teller in New York and other cities, Joseph Magnin in San Francisco, Giorgio's of Beverly Hills, Marshall Field in Chicago, and Sara Fredericks of Palm Beach.

After retiring from MGM in 1966, Rose designed for movies on a limited free-lance basis. She must have realized that the importance of movie designers was diminishing, and wisely chose to rest on her glittering laurels. By then she had more than lived up to the prophetic lines next to her grammar school graduation picture:

> *Helen is our great designer*
> *Prizes by the score had she—*
> *She's the designer of our fashions*
> *From dressing gowns, to gowns for*
>   *tea.*

Irene Sharaff (right) giving last minute instructions in MGM's workroom to the head wardrobe fitter, as they inspect one of the gowns that was designed for The Secret Life of Walter Mitty *(1947).*

IRENE SHARAFF

BETWEEN 1951 AND 1969, IRENE SHARAFF RECEIVED FIVE ACADEMY AWARDS and nine nominations for best costume design. They were well-earned recognition for a consummate artist, who also includes painting and sculpting among her talents.

Sharaff's career began in 1928, when she was a teenage art student in New York. Eva Le Gallienne, founder and managing director of the Civic Repertory Theatre, hired Sharaff to serve as a costume designer, scenic draftsman, prop assistant, and occasional crowd-scene extra for Civic's brilliant productions of the classics. For the first six months the company's budget was so limited that Sharaff worked for room and board alone. Those times were busy, often hectic, and demanded a high degree of creativity on a shoestring. She learned how to turn curtain and lampshade fabrics found at bargain counters into pirate costumes for *Peter Pan* and peasant blouses for *The Cherry Orchard*; brass toilet chains from a hardware store became gold necklaces in *Romeo and Juliet*.

By 1931, Sharaff had saved enough money to fulfill her dream of spending a year in Paris—an experience that had a profound influence on her work. She was particularly impressed by the theatrical designs of the painters Christian Bérard, Pavel Tchelitchew, and André Derain. But most of all, she discovered the subtleties of French couture. From the collections of designers such as

A drawing by Irene Sharaff of a piper for MGM's 1954 version of the musical Brigadoon. *Sharaff's talent as a painter has made her costume sketches collectors' items.*

Chanel and Schiaparelli she learned what perfection means in terms of design and the finish of clothes, and she later exacted the same standards in the execution of her own work.

When she returned to New York, Sharaff picked up where she had left off, designing costumes for the Civic Repertory. Her first production, *Alice in Wonderland*, brought her the Donaldson Award for costumes and scenery. Astutely, she had based her designs on John Tenniel's original illustrations for Lewis Carroll's fantasy. After that Sharaff's career took off, and for the next decade she designed a number of Broadway shows and ballets. First she did the "Easter Parade" number that Irving Berlin wrote for Hassard Short's new production of *As Thousands Cheer*. Working exclusively with various tones of brown, sepia, umber, sienna, and taupe, Sharaff recreated a stage rotogravure of an Easter Sunday fashion parade that resembled a page from the *New York Times* in 1885. The startlingly imaginative effect established the young designer as one of the theater's most promising talents.

Other productions she designed during the thirties included Rodgers and Hart's *On Your Toes* (1936), with Ray Bolger and Tamara Geva dancing George Balanchine's balletic love-tragedy. The decorative starkness of the costumes so impressed the noted choreographer that he later sent Sharaff many other commissions. In 1941, Sharaff costumed *Lady in the Dark*, with Gertrude Lawrence, and the following year she did *By Jupiter* and also created stylish G-strings and strip-tease raiment for the voluptuous Gypsy Rose Lee in *Star and Garter*.

Sharaff's call to Hollywood came in 1942, from Arthur Freed at MGM. Freed wanted Sharaff to be part of a unit that created costumes for musicals, a profit-

As Kate in The Taming of the Shrew *(Columbia, 1967), Elizabeth Taylor was never more beautiful, thanks to her favorite costume designer. Sharaff's work for* The Shrew *is among the most definitive Shakespearean costuming ever done for the screen.*

Irene Sharaff was able to transform the exquisite Elizabeth Taylor into the frumpiest of stars for Warner Brothers' version of Edward Albee's Who's Afraid of Virginia Woolf? *(1966). With clever padding in the wrong places, Sharaff contrived to make the usually glamorous Miss Taylor take on the appearance of the aging, overweight, disenchanted character Taylor courageously assumed. The slacks and misshapen jacket provided her by Sharaff, and seen in this photograph, illustrate how a designer can literally re-create an actress to fit a script's required image. The length of the jacket and sleeves—awkward, cut at a point that can only more cruelly accentuate Taylor's already overpadded hips—is an example of professional know-how.*

able studio specialty. At the time of her arrival in Hollywood, however, no musical was scheduled for production, so Sharaff was assigned the dramatic scenario of *Madame Curie* (1943), with Greer Garson and Walter Pidgeon. Deceptively simple, Sharaff's perfectly evoked period costumes for that film revealed her talent for designing realistic clothing as well as she did fantasy gowns.

Sharaff's first musical for MGM was *Meet Me in St. Louis* (1944). It was produced by Arthur Freed, directed by Vincente Minnelli, and starred Judy Garland, Mary Astor, and Margaret O'Brien. Again the designer demonstrated her ability to create period pieces by turning out the kind of elaborate frills-and-lace costumes that delighted movie audiences. The film firmly established Sharaff's reputation in Hollywood as well as her position at MGM. Most of her subsequent film work was done there, although she also did a number of movies for other studios.

Her next films included *Yolanda and the Thief* (1945), *The Best Years of Our Lives* (1946), *Ziegfeld Follies* (1946, with Helen Rose), and *An American In Paris* (1951, with Orry-Kelly and Walter Plunkett). For the scenery and costumes of the ballet scene between Leslie Caron and Gene Kelly in the latter film, Sharaff won her first Academy Award. Then she costumed *Call Me Madam* (1953), *Brigadoon* (1954), *A Star Is Born* (1954), *Guys and Dolls* (1955), *The King and I* (1956, Academy Award), *Porgy and Bess* (1959), *Can-Can* (1960), *West Side Story* (1961, Academy Award), and *Flower Drum Song* (1961). She also dressed Elizabeth Taylor in *Cleopatra* (1963, Academy Award), *The Sandpiper* (1965), *Who's Afraid of Virginia Woolf?* (1966, Academy Award), and *The Taming of the Shrew* (1967).

To achieve historical accuracy in *Cleopatra*, research for the outfits was done from early Egyptian bas-reliefs, tomb paintings, and sculpture. Miss Taylor was so impressed by Sharaff's work that she asked the designer to create the dress for her wedding to Richard Burton. It was a softly pleated silk jersey gown of primrose yellow.

Barbra Streisand also benefited from Sharaff's talents in *Funny Girl* (1968) and *Hello, Dolly* (1969). The designer then did *Justine* (1969), *The Great White Hope* (1970), *The Way We Were* (1973), and *The Other Side of Midnight* (1976).

During her break from Hollywood, Sharaff devoted most of her time to painting and sculpture, with only an occasional sortie into designing for the New York theater and ballet. Never interested in publicity or the sort of exploitation that is generally made of a successful career in the movies, Irene Sharaff continues to remain a private person.

But the thirty-odd films that bear her name, her awards, and the number of her former assistants who are now designers in their own right speak eloquently of Sharaff's art and her example. She combines a remarkable understanding of theater, dance, and film and is equally at home in period and modern settings. Perhaps what makes Sharaff's work so distinctive is its intelligence and no-nonsense realism. Her costumes are always perfectly researched and functional, never overpowering or inhibiting, yet exquisitely crafted. Such versatility, style, and care have well deserved more than one Academy Award.

ACADEMY AWARD WINNERS FOR COSTUME DESIGN

1948	Roger K. Furse	black-and-white	*Hamlet*	Universal-International
	Dorothy Jeakins Karinska	color	*Joan of Arc*	Walter Wanger
1949	Edith Head Giles Steele	black-and-white	*The Heiress*	Paramount
	Leah Rhodes Travilla Marjorie Best	color	*Adventures of Don Juan*	Warner Brothers
1950	Edith Head Charles LeMaire	black-and-white	*All About Eve*	Twentieth Century-Fox
	Edith Head Dorothy Jeakins Eloise Jenssen Giles Steele Gwen Wakeling	color	*Samson and Delilah*	Paramount
1951	Edith Head	black-and-white	*A Place in the Sun*	Paramount
	Orry-Kelly Walter Plunkett Irene Sharaff	color	*An American in Paris*	Metro-Goldwyn-Mayer
1952	Helen Rose	black-and-white	*The Bad and the Beautiful*	Metro-Goldwyn-Mayer
	Marcel Vertes	color	*Moulin Rouge*	Romulus–United Artists

1953	Edith Head	black-and-white	*Roman Holiday*	Paramount
	Charles LeMaire Emile Santiago	color	*The Robe*	Twentieth Century-Fox
1954	Edith Head	black-and-white	*Sabrina*	Paramount
	Sanzo Wada	color	*Gate of Hell*	Daiei Productions (Japan)
1955	Helen Rose	black-and-white	*I'll Cry Tomorrow*	Metro- Goldwyn- Mayer
	Charles LeMaire	color	*Love Is a Many-Splendored Thing*	Twentieth Century-Fox
1956	Jean Louis	black-and-white	*The Solid Gold Cadillac*	Columbia
	Irene Sharaff	color	*The King and I*	Twentieth Century-Fox
1957	Orry-Kelly	color	*Les Girls*	Metro- Goldwyn- Mayer
1958	Cecil Beaton	color	*Gigi*	Metro- Goldwyn- Mayer
1959	Orry-Kelly	black-and-white	*Some Like It Hot*	United Artists
	Elizabeth Haffenden	color	*Ben Hur*	Metro- Goldwyn- Mayer
1960	Edith Head Edward Stevenson	black-and-white	*The Facts of Life*	Paramount
	Valles Bill Thomas	color	*Spartacus*	Universal

1961	Piero Gherardi	black-and-white	*La Dolce Vita*	Riama Film Productions (Italy; dist. Astor Pictures)
	Irene Sharaff	color	*West Side Story*	Mirisch–United Artists
1962	Norman Koch	black-and-white	*What Ever Happened to Baby Jane?*	Warner Brothers–Seven Arts
	Mary Wills	color	*The Wonderful World of the Brothers Grimm*	Metro-Goldwyn-Mayer
1963	Piero Gherardi	black-and-white	*8 1/2*	Cineriz Productions (Italy; dist. Embassy Pictures)
	Irene Sharaff Nino Novarese Renie	color	*Cleopatra*	Twentieth Century-Fox
1964	Dorothy Jeakins	black-and-white	*The Night of the Iguana*	Metro-Goldwyn-Mayer–Seven Arts
	Cecil Beaton	color	*My Fair Lady*	Warner Brothers
1965	Julie Harris	black-and-white	*Darling*	Embassy
	Phyllis Dalton	color	*Doctor Zhivago*	Ponti–Metro-Goldwyn-Mayer
1966	Irene Sharaff	black-and-white	*Who's Afraid of Virginia Woolf?*	Warner Brothers
	Elizabeth Haffenden Joan Bridge	color	*A Man for All Seasons*	Columbia

1967	John Truscott	color	*Camelot*	Warner Brothers
1968	Danilo Donati	color	*Romeo and Juliet*	Paramount–BHE–Verona–Dino de Laurentis
1969	Margaret Furse	color	*Anne of the Thousand Days*	Wallis-Universal
1970	Nino Novarese	color	*Cromwell*	Columbia
1971	Yvonne Blake Antonio Castillo	color	*Nicholas and Alexandra*	Horizon-Columbia
1972	Anthony Powell	color	*Travels with My Aunt*	Metro-Goldwyn-Mayer
1973	Edith Head	color	*The Sting*	Zanuck-Brown-Universal
1974	Theoni V. Aldredge	color	*The Great Gatsby*	Paramount
1975	Ulla-Britt Soderlund Milena Canonero	color	*Barry Lyndon*	Warner Brothers
1976	Danilo Donati	color	*Fellini's Casanova*	Alberto Grimaldi–Universal
1977	John Mollo	color	*Star Wars*	Twentieth Century-Fox
1978	Anthony Powell	color	*Death on the Nile*	Paramount
1979	Albert Wolsky	color	*All That Jazz*	Twentieth Century-Fox–Columbia

A SELECTED
BIBLIOGRAPHY

GENERAL

AMORY, CLEVELAND, and Frederic Bradlee. *Vanity Fair: Selections from America's Most Memorable Magazine. A Cavalcade of the 1920's and 1930's.* New York: Viking, 1960.

BAINBRIDGE, JOHN. *Garbo.* New York: Doubleday, 1955.

BAXTER, JOHN. *Hollywood in the Thirties.* New York: A. S. Barnes, 1968.

BLUM, DANIEL. *A Pictorial History of the Silent Screen.* New York: Putnam's, 1953.

BODEEN, DE WITT. "Nazimova." *Films in Review,* December 1972.

CARR, LARRY. *Four Fabulous Faces: Swanson, Garbo, Crawford, Dietrich.* New York: Galahad Books, 1970.

CARTER, RANDOLPH. *The World of Flo Ziegfeld.* New York and Washington, D.C.: Praeger, 1974.

CHIERICHETTI, DAVID. *Hollywood Costume Design.* New York: Harmony Books, 1976.

CONWAY, MICHAEL, and Mark Ricci. *The Films of Jean Harlow.* New York: Bonanza Books, 1965.

CROCE, ARLENE. *The Fred Astaire and Ginger Rogers Book.* New York: A Sunrise Book, Dutton, 1972.

CURTIS, ANTHONY. *The Rise and Fall of the Matinee Idol.* New York: St. Martin's, 1974.

EELLS, GEORGE. *Ginger, Loretta and Irene Who?* New York: Putnam's, 1976.

————. *Hedda and Louella.* New York: Putnam's, 1972.

EMBODEN, WILLIAM. *Sarah Bernhardt.* London: Studio Vista, a division of Cassell and Collier Macmillan Publishers, Ltd., 1974.

FLORA, PAUL. *Vivat Vamp.* London: Dobson Books, Ltd., 1965.

FLUDAS, JOHN. *"Fatal Women." Opera News*, February 12, 1977.

GALLICO, PAUL, and Nickolas Murray. *The Revealing Eye: Personalities of the 1920's.* New York: Atheneum, 1967.

GASLAND, MADGE, Madeleine Ginsberg, Martin Bathersly, Valerie Lloyd, and Ivor Davis. *Fashion 1900–1939.* London: Idea Books International, 1975.

GISH, LILLIAN. *Dorothy and Lillian Gish.* New York: Scribners, 1973.

GRIFFITH, RICHARD. *The Talkies: Articles and Illustrations from Photoplay Magazine 1928–1940.* New York: Dover, 1971.

GRIFFITH, RICHARD, and Arthur Mayer. *The Movies: The Sixty-Year Story of the World of Hollywood and Its Effects in America from Pre-Nickelodeon Days to the Present.* New York: Simon and Schuster, 1957.

GUILES, FRED LAWRENCE. *Marion Davies.* New York: McGraw-Hill, 1972.

HARRIS, WARREN G. *Gable and Lombard.* New York: Simon and Schuster, 1974.

HIGHAM, CHARLES. *Cecil B. De Mille: A Biography of the Most Successful Film Maker of Them All.* New York: Scribners, 1973.

HOPPER, HEDDA, and James Brough. *The Whole Truth and Nothing But.* New York: Doubleday, 1963.

HOWELL, GEORGINA. *In Vogue: Sixty Years of International Celebrities and Fashion from British Vogue.* New York: Schocken, 1976.

HUDSON, RICHARD. *60 Years of Vamps and Camps.* New York: Drake, 1973.

HUDSON, RICHARD, and Raymond Lee. *Gloria Swanson.* New York: Castle Books, A. S. Barnes, 1970.

KOBAL, JOHN. *Hollywood Glamour Portraits: 145 Photos of Stars 1926–1949.* New York: Dover, 1976.

————. *Marlene Dietrich.* New York: Dutton, 1968.

KNIGHT, ARTHUR. *The Warner Brothers Golden Anniversary Book.* New York: A Dell Special, Film and Venture Corporation, 1973.

KUHNS, WILLIAM. *Movies in America.* Dayton, Ohio: Pflaum/Standard, 1972.

LAVER, JAMES. *Women's Dress in the Jazz Age.* London: Hamish Hamilton, Ltd., 1964.

LAWTON, RICHARD. *A World of Movies: 70 Years of Film History.* New York: Dell, 1974.

LEARY, LIAM. *The Silent Cinema.* New York: Dutton, 1965.

LEESE, ELIZABETH. *Costume Design in the Movies.* Isle of Wight, Eng.: BCW Publishing, Ltd., 1976.

LEVIN, MARTIN. *Hollywood and the Great Fan Magazines.* New York: Arbor House, 1970.

MARILLIER, H. C. *The Early Work of Aubrey Beardsley.* New York: Dover, 1967.

McCONATHY, DALE, and Diana Vreeland. *Hollywood Costume.* New York: Harry N. Abrams, in cooperation with the Metropolitan Museum of Art, 1976.

MURRAY, KEN. *The Golden Days of San Simeon.* New York: Doubleday, 1969.

NEGRI, POLA. *Memoirs of a Star.* New York: Doubleday, 1970.

PARISH, JAMES ROBERT. *The Paramount Pretties.* Secaucus, N.J.: Castle Books, Arlington House, 1972.

PARSONS, LOUELLA. *Tell It to Louella.* New York: Putnam's, 1961.

PRATT, WILLIAM. *Scarlett Fever: The Ultimate Pictorial Treasury of Gone With the Wind.* New York: Macmillan, 1977.

ROBINSON, DAVID. *Hollywood in the Twenties.* New York: Tantivy Press, in association with A. Zwemmer, Ltd., and A. S. Barnes, 1968.

SCAGNETTI, JACK. *The Intimate Life of Rudolph Valentino.* New York: Jonathan David, 1975.

SENNETT, TED. *The Movie Buff's Book*. New York: Pyramid Books, 1975.

SHULMAN, IRVING. *Harlow: An Intimate Biography*. New York: Bernard Geis, 1964.

SKINNER, CORNELIA OTIS. *Madame Sarah*. New York: Dell, 1968.

SPENCER, CHARLES. *The World of Serge Diaghilev*. London: Penguin Books, Ltd., 1974.

SPRINGER, JOHN. *All Talking, All Singing, All Dancing*. New York: Citadel, 1966.

STALLINGS, PENNY, and Howard Mandelbaum. *Flesh and Fantasy*. New York: St. Martin's, 1978.

STINE, WHITNEY, and Bette Davis. *Mother Goddam*. New York: Hawthorn Books, 1974.

TAYLOR, DEEMS, Marcelene Peterson, and Bryant Hale. *A Pictorial History of the Movies*. New York: Simon and Schuster, 1950.

THOMAS, BOB. *Selznick*. New York: Doubleday, 1970.

TRENT, PAUL. *The Image Makers: Sixty Years of Hollywood Glamour*. New York: McGraw-Hill, 1972.

ZUKOR, ADOLPH, and Dale Kramer. *The Public Is Never Wrong: The Autobiography of Adolph Zukor*. New York: Putnam's, 1953.

DESIGNER-RELATED BOOKS

BAILLEN, CLAUDE. *Chanel Solitaire*. New York: Quadrangle, New York Times Book Company, 1974.

BEATON, CECIL. *Cecil Beaton's Fair Lady*. London: Weidenfeld and Nicolson, Ltd., 1964.

———. *The Face of The World: An International Scrap Book of People and Places*. New York: John Day, n. d.

———. *The Wandering Years 1922–1939*. Boston: Little, Brown, 1961.

ERTÉ. *Designs by Erté: Fashion Drawings and Illustrations from Harper's Bazaar*. New York: Dover, 1976.

———. *Erté Fashions*. London/New York: Academy Editions and St. Martin's, 1972.

———. *Things I Remember*. New York: Quadrangle, New York Times Book Company, 1975.

GREER, HOWARD. *Designing Male*. New York: Putnam's, 1949.

HAEDRICH, MARCEL. *Coco Chanel: Her Life, Her Secrets*. Boston/Toronto: Little, Brown, 1972.

HEAD, EDITH, and Jane Kesner Ardmore. *The Dress Doctor*. Boston/Toronto: Little, Brown, 1959.

LEE, SARAH TOMERLIN, ed. *American Fashion: The Life and Lines of Adrian, Mainbocher, McCardell, Norell, Trigère*. New York: Quadrangle, New York Times Book Company, 1975.

LYNAM, RUTH. *Couture: An Illustrated History of the Great Paris Designers and Their Creations*. New York: Doubleday, 1972.

ROSE, HELEN. *Just Make Them Beautiful*. Santa Monica, Calif.: Dennis-Landman, 1976.

SHARAFF, IRENE. *Broadway and Hollywood: Costumes Designed by Irene Sharaff*. New York: Van Nostrand Reinhold, 1976.

SPENCER, CHARLES. *Erté*. New York: Clarkson N. Potter, 1970.

WHITE, PALMER. *Poiret*. New York: Clarkson N. Potter, 1973.

INDEX

of gown for, *228*; Rose designs for, 121,
124, 237, 239; Sharaff designs for, *139*,
142, *243*, *244*
Taylor, Ruth, *65*
Technicolor, 80–81
television: impact on motion picture
production, 106, 109, 137; old movie
couples on, *154–57*
Temple, Shirley: Royer design for, *88*, 90
Thalberg, Mr. and Mrs. Irving, 42; feud
with Hearst, 52–53. *See also* Shearer,
Norma
Tirtoff, Roman de. *See* Erté
Tosi, Piero, 149
Tracy, Spencer, *122*
Travilla, William, and Monroe, Marilyn,
119, *120*
Truscott, John, designs for *Camelot* by, 147,
148
Tuffin (couturier), 126
Turner, Lana: Rose designs for, 121, *122*,
123, 127, 237
Twentieth Century-Fox: and Banton, Travis,
90, 171, 177, 179; and Herschel, 88; and
LeMaire, Charles, 90; and Monroe,
Marilyn, 117, 119; and musicals, 127–28;
and Orry-Kelly, 220–21, 224; and Rose,
Helen, 236; and Royer and Wakeling, 88,
90; and Stevenson, Edward, 93; use of
free-lance designers by, 84

Universal: and Greer, Howard, 199–200; and
Head, Edith, 151; and West, Vera, 90
Urban, Joseph, 17
used costumes: collectors and, 152;
remodeled or reused during World War II,
104. *See also* Metropolitan Museum of Art

Valentino, Rudolph, *14*
vamp, the, 10
Van Runkle, Theadora: designs for *Bonnie
and Clyde* by, 147–48, *149*; film credits of,
148–49

Velles, J. Arlington, 215
Vertès, Marcel, 127
Vionnet, 13
Vreeland, Diana, *158*

Wakeling, Gwen, 84, 88, 116; designs for
Grapes of Wrath by, 99
Walton, Tony, 149
wardrobe departments, 16, 27–28
wardrobe plot, 29–30, *31*
Warner Brothers: and musicals, 79–80;
formation of, 15; by mid-1970s, 152; and
Newman, Bernard, 93; and Orry-Kelly,
28, 71–75, 105, 219, 221
Wayne, John, *102*
wedding gowns: by Greer, Howard, *195*; by
Head, Edith, 105, *108*; by Rose, Helen,
121, *122*, 237, 239; by Sharaff, Irene, 245
West, Claire, 16; design by, *18*; and Greer,
Howard, 195
West, Mae, 24; Banton designs for, *32*, *47*,
171, *176*, 179; Head designs for, 206, 210;
Schiaparelli designs for, 77–78, *79*;
duplicate costumes for, 31
West, Vera, 43; designs by, *89*, *103*; film
credits, 90; and Greer, Howard, 200; at
Universal, 90
West Side Story, 137, *138*, 139
Western Costume Company, 28, 153
Williams, Esther: Rose bathing suit for, 121,
124
Wizard of Oz, The, 81, *88*
World War II, 100, 104–6
Worth (designer), 13

Young, Loretta, 55, 214, 216; Irene design
for, *60*; Royer and Wakeling designs for,
88, 90

Zukor, Adolph, 3, 4–5, 15, 26, 38, 170, 179;
and Banton's use of furs, 64; Paramount's
one-hundredth birthday party for, 153. *See
also* Paramount

JSC Willey Library
337 College Hill
Johnson, VT 05656

JSC Willey Library
337 College Hill
Johnson, VT 05656